Tough to Reach, Tough to Teach

Students with Behavior Problems

Sylvia Rockwell, Ph.D.

Council for Exceptional Children
The voice and vision of special education

Library of Congress Cataloging-in-Publication Data

Rockwell, Sylvia.
      Tough to reach, tough to teach : students with behavior problems/
by Sylvia Rockwell.
        P. cm.
      Includes index
      ISBN 0-86586-235-4
      1. Problem children—Education—United States.
      2. Classroom management—United States.
      3. Behavior modification—United States
   1. Title.
   LC4802.R63 1993
   371.93—dc20

           92-43363
           CIP

ISBN 0-86586-235-4
ISBN 0-86586-427-6 (Second edition, revised and expanded)
Copyright 1993 by The Council for Exceptional Children, 1110 N. Glebe Rd, Suite 300, Arlington, Virginia 22201

Stock No. P5773
First edition 1993
Second edition 2006

Printed in the United States of America

10 9 8 7 6 5 4 3 2 1

This book is dedicated with love and appreciation to my husband, John. His belief in me helped me begin this book. His willingness to take on added household chores allowed me to complete it.

Kala, Donnie, and Jesse are mentioned with love and thanks for the times they not only let Mom work, but also were overheard telling their friends about this book with a shared sense of excitement.

John Rieser and Duque Wilson are mentioned for their loving, nurturing guidance. For almost 20 years, they have served as mentors and friends.

For all past, present, and future students, a special thanks is in order. Their courage and strength are a constant source of wonder and inspiration.

And last, but not least, a thanks to Dr. Eleanor Guetzloe for her wonderful support, professional guidance, and positive approach.

Contents

Foreword

The Council for Exceptional Children (CEC) is committed to publishing resources produced by teachers for teachers. This work, by Sylvia Rockwell, Ph.D. who taught in a school for students with severe behavioral problems, is certain to be welcomed by teachers who work with disruptive students. In this highly readable text, Dr. Rockwell offers practical suggestions for managing behaviors that can be difficult even for highly experienced teachers. Profanity, fighting, tantrums, and resistance are all behaviors that make kids "tough to reach and tough to teach."

The vignettes used by Dr. Rockwell to illustrate various classroom challenges are, unfortunately, all too familiar to teachers in contemporary classrooms. Children do not have to be classified "emotionally disturbed" or "behaviorally disordered" to act out when under stress. Being prepared is half the battle, and this resource will help every teacher be better prepared to teach students better ways to communicate.

Dr. Rockwell's experiences with children with behavioral problems range from intensive, round-the-clock teaching and supervision in wilderness camp settings to traditional classroom teaching. She has also worked with students who are gifted. She received the "Teacher of the Year Award" from Calvin A. Hunsinger School in 1991, the "Distinguished Alumni Award" from Okaloosa Walton Junior College in 1990, and the Council for Children with Behavioral Disorders' Professional Performance Award in 1994. We are proud to count Dr. Rockwell among the members of CEC. We appreciate her contribution to improving educational outcomes for students with exceptionalities and in assisting professionals with this resource to enhance effective professional practice.

1

Introduction

The anecdotal sections represent typical classroom events with students who present behavioral concerns. Although some of the language in this book may be offensive, it is included only to illustrate the reality of some of the challenges teachers and their students face. While it is disconcerting to hear abusive language from such young students, it is comforting to have a plan in mind to deal with the important task of teaching students more effective ways to communicate. The following anecdote introduces children who require individual attention to their social, emotional, behavioral, and academic needs in order to become fully functioning members of their classrooms, schools, and communities.

ANECDOTE

The morning sun filters through a haze of fog as a cool breeze rustles the fallen leaves. A deceptively soothing stage is set for the day's adventure. Like Pandora's box, the opening of the bus doors brings a swarm of frantic activity.

My few moments of quiet reflection are broken as bus 825 pulls into the driveway of DKJ Elementary School. Before the bus has come to a complete stop, I am standing, straining to get a clue as to the atmosphere inside the bus. As the doors open, several children are already out of their seats, feet scuffling, book bags slapping against backs and backrests. Voices rise in anger or joyfully acknowledge another's anger. The bus driver gives me the thumbs down sign and shakes her head.

Lydel is the first one off the bus. He's almost 10 years old, but he has experienced more tragedy than most adults. Family members have been killed in his presence. Drug abuse, sexual abuse, and frequent changes in guardians, along with impoverished living conditions, have taken their toll on his sense of reality, self-respect, and trust. Lydel experiences hallucinations when not kept on medication. Voices, which he describes as his protection, tell him who will hurt him so he can attack before the other person has a chance to strike first or even defend himself. Medication controls the voices and the unexpected attacks that accompany them. Only time and a lot of work will make a dent in his sense of self-control and trust.

Next in line is Tomika, our only girl. Tomika is 8 years old, looks younger, and acts as if she were 28. Of all our children, she is the most exceptional at controlling her classmates. On a good day, she can be very helpful—a busy mother hen soothing over arguments, reprimanding those who forget class rules, and cajoling reluctant classmates into compliance. The boys vie for her special attention. She loves it and uses them unmercifully. On bad days, she leads them into any inappropriate behavior she can conjure up. Money, food, and promises of extra attention are just a few of the incentives she's been known to use with peers to pit them against each other and those in authority over them. Adults are Tomika's most difficult dilemma. She desperately wants their love and protection, and just as desperately wants to maintain the upper hand.

Tommy's booksack flies over Tomika's head and rolls across the sidewalk before his slight body becomes visible in the doorway. I approach cautiously from the side and hear Tommy's slurred speech and cries as the bus driver holds his hands and tries to calm him. The other children, on and off the bus, explode into laughter and rounds of teasing remarks. Tommy is our youngest, mentally, emotionally, physically, and socially. He was taken from his biological mother when he was 4 years old because of neglect. Even after 3 years in foster care, he still suffers from the effects of the neglect in obvious ways, such as hearing and speech difficulties, and in harder to access areas, such as emotional immaturity and poor impulse control.

"Tommy, come on now and get your book sack." Tommy pulls away from the bus driver, jumps down the steps, and draws back his fist, threatening to punch Lydel, who is rolling on the sidewalk, kicking his feet and howling with laughter.

"Look at the baby!"

"Lydel. Get up. Help Tommy and yourself by lining up." Without taking a breath, I turn to Tommy. "Tommy. Hands at your sides."

"Everyone is laughing at me."

"It's time to line up, Tommy. Get your book sack."

I keep an eye on Tommy, Lydel, and Tomika as Kevin, Marcus, and Jonathan file off the bus in varying stages of distress due to the confusion.

Kevin's biological mother abused drugs while she was pregnant with him. He was hospitalized during his first few months of life for malnutrition and allergies. Since infancy, he has lived in a single foster home with parents who have one child of their own. Kevin has an insatiable need for attention and is easily frustrated, but he is manageable in small group settings as long as his need for recognition is met frequently and positively.

Marcus is verbally and physically aggressive. His body is solid and strong. Profanity, threats, and actual physical attacks are so much a part of his behavior that I wonder whether he ever has time to relax and be an 8-year-old boy. What happened to the child behind that "macho man" facade? According to school records, he is the only child in the class with an intact family. Other than the fact that he is the baby of the family, his mother has no clue as to the origin of his adjustment problems.

"Good morning, Kevin and Marcus."

"Hi, Mrs. R. Did you see what Tommy did?"

"Yes, Kevin. Please help him by getting in line."

"What'd you say? I didn't do nothing!" Marcus yells, jerking his shoulders back.

"Good morning, Marcus." I smile, hoping he'll read the nonverbal cues and relax a little.

"Oh . . . Hi." He looks at me guardedly over his shoulder as I turn to check on Jonathan.

Jonathan is doing well. He goes to regular classes for 2 to 3 hours a day. We are trying to ease him into full-time mainstreaming. Unlike the others, Jonathan has never been as much of a threat to others as he has been to himself. Multiple divorces and parental bouts of drug addiction took a toll on his early development. Low self-esteem and fears combined to paralyze him. He became easy prey for more aggressive classmates, who could reduce him to tears, screaming, and anguished writhing on the floor with little more than a whispered threat. As Jonathan's parents struggled to overcome their own difficulties, Jonathan began his journey. Learning to be assertive in a healthy, self-respecting manner was essential to any future success.

"Hello, Jonathan."

"Hey, Mrs. Rockwell, I got my homework."

"Great, Jonathan! We'll look at it in the room. OK?"

"OK. What's wrong with Tommy?"

"He's upset right now. Let's line up. Kevin is the leader today."

"Mrs. R., Lydel and Tommy won't get in line."

Welcome to the world of teaching students with behavior problems. In public school settings, these children are described as exhibiting extremely inappropriate behavior given the situation and stimulus. Their behavior interferes with their academic progress but is not a result of low IQ or any physical impairment such as deafness. This description is neat, unemotional, and totally operational. It does nothing to prepare the unsuspecting, uninitiated adult for the reality of daily life in the classroom. Emotions run high. Stress, if not dealt with constructively, takes its toll on the children and the teacher. Energy, enthusiasm, and a tolerance for ambiguity are the teacher's first lines of defense. The children will curse, physically attack, criticize real and imagined limitations, and test adults and each other to the very edge of decency and integrity. They will need and expect the teacher's intelligent, humane, and professional best in response to the worst they can muster. Why would a basically gentle, capable, well-educated person submit himself or herself to such treatment on a daily basis for 10 months out of the year? The need for a challenge is one reason, along with the feeling of awe when given the privilege of watching children grow in their sense of self-confidence, self-control, and trust in others. These students are not incapable of learning. If behavior problems did not exist, they would be average or above-average students. Their failure to master academic material is a manifestation of other, more pressing problems.

After writing this book 12 years ago, I considered throwing it away. The rapid advances in technology had opened doors to our understanding of learning problems and emotional and behavioral disorders through gene and brain research. I thoroughly expected the content of books like this to be obsolete within a few years. Medical professionals would be able to fix childhood disorders with gene splicing, medication, tiny electrodes implanted in the brain, and surgery. We were then and continue to be even now on the brink of many awe-inspiring discoveries. Since those days of doubt about the usefulness of books on managing classroom behavior, however, I have come to understand that the medical profession still has years of research to conduct before the world I envision for children's mental and physical health becomes a reality. Society's response to children in need of mental health services is yet another hurdle to be overcome.

Teachers, administrators, parents, and concerned members of the general public will continue to seek answers to questions about how to best meet these children's needs until medical science uncovers significant mysteries surrounding human growth and development and until society as a whole embraces these children with the compassion they deserve.

For too many years we have blamed parents, teachers, and children themselves for the challenges their differences in development have created. Mothers of children with Autism, for example, were once blamed for their children's inabilities to connect with others. Doctors noticed that the mothers did not engage their babies in eye contact and cuddling. Later doctors discovered that mothers had quit trying to force their babies to engage in behaviors that were beyond their abilities. Many conditions formerly believed to be learned behaviors alone have come to be understood as having a biological origin such as Tourette's Syndrome, obsessive compulsive disorder, bi-polar disorder, and attention deficit hyperactivity disorder. This second edition of *Tough to Reach, Tough to Teach: Students with Behavior Problems* includes updated research on (a) instructional strategies; (b) behavior management interventions, (c) online resources for educators, parents, and students; (d) guidelines for establishing a curriculum of hope and resilience; and (e) suggestions for effectively advocating for an often misunderstood group.

Someday in the not too distant future, I do believe that scientists will unlock the secret chemical codes that lead to learning difficulties and mental illness. I dream of a day when children no longer suffer, parents are no longer blamed, and books like this gather dust in some moldy, unused corner of the library. Until then, we who seek to support children others have rejected must join hands. We must stop the blame game. Our energies need to be focused on (a) skillful application of research-based best practices; and (b) advocacy at local, state, regional, and national levels.

2

Classroom Climate

ANECDOTE

"1 ... 2 ... 3 ... Great! I see Kevin in line. Thank you, Tomika. Look at Lydel and Jonathan! Good job, Marcus! Tommy, I see you have your booksack now. Please get in line."

"Let's just go. He's a baby!"

"We need to help Tommy make a good decision, Lydel."

"OK," Lydel says grudgingly, "Come on, Tommy. Line up with me." "Thank you, Lydel."

"Tommy, what is your decision? Will you line up on your own or do you want me to hold your hand?"

With a silent, murderous look, Tommy jerks himself into line, and we began the walk back to the classroom.

Setting a healthy, productive classroom climate begins before the children come through the door. Five basic components of classroom climate are (a) setting limits, (b) safety, (c) trust, (d) acceptance, and (e) a sense of purpose (Redl, 1966; Driekers, Grumwald, & Pepper, Glasser, 1998; Jones, 1993). These components are illustrated throughout the anecdotes as well as through direct explanations of terms, strategies, and interventions.

Positive Behavior Support (PBS) is a systemic approach to applying research-based best practices to develop, implement, and monitor behavior management plans at the school-wide, classroom, and individual levels (Lewis,& Sugai, 1999; Scott & Nelson, 1999; Sprick, Sprick, & Garrison, 1992). Classroom level components of PBS are defined as (a) proactive strategies designed to avoid unnecessary problems, (b) classroom expectations, (c) rules, (d) routines or procedures, (e) educative interventions designed to teach desired behaviors and skills, (f) reinforcement, and (g) planned responses to noncompliance. Behavior management, classroom management, and instruction are included in the overall assessment of the classroom as well as the implementation of strategies or interventions in response to students' needs. The chart provided below illustrates the how PBS and the five basic components of classroom management described in this book are related. Integrating information from diverse research foundations (behavioral, cognitive-behavioral, and ecological) extends the menu of options for addressing problem behaviors while maintaining the integrity of the overall classroom-wide and individual level intervention plans.

Integration of PBS with Components of Classroom Climate

	Setting Limits	Safety	Trust	Acceptance	Sense of Purpose
Expectations	X	X	X	X	X
Proactive Environmental Strategies	X	X		X	X
Rules	X	X			X
Routines/ Procedures	X	X			X
Educative Behavioral Strategies	X	X	X	X	X
Educative Academic Strategies			X	X	X
Reinforcement			X	X	X
Responses to Noncompliance	X	X	X	X	X

SETTING LIMITS

Establishing limits in the classroom includes the consideration of expectations, rules, routines or procedures, plans for responding to noncompliance, and strategies for teaching desired behaviors. Simply telling students what is expected is insufficient. Some students speak English as a second language. Others have processing deficits that do not allow them to remember what they hear for more than a few moments. A percentage of students in any given classroom will have mental health problems—many will be undiagnosed. Assuming that all students understand the posted expectations in the same way is unrealistic. Cultural and socio-economic differences in students' backgrounds affect their understanding of concepts such as respect, kindness, and cooperation. Each student may have a different idea of how to demonstrate those values. Misunderstandings could easily occur. An example from my own childhood illustrates this point.

ANECDOTE

When I was young, our family moved often. During most of my elementary school years I began the school term in one town and ended it in another. In the northern states where I began my formal education, I was taught to answer adults with "Yes" or "No." "Yeah" and "nope" or "naw" were considered disrespectful. I never talked that way to an elder. Early on my first day of school in Alabama after having been attending school in Seattle, Washington, my teacher asked me a question. I don't remember to this day what she asked. I do remember clearly what happened when I answered her in my most respectful and quiet voice with, "Yes." She began to yell, became quite red in the face, and made it clear that I was never to speak to her in that way again. She asked if I understood her. I did not understand why she was angry, but did want to convey my respect for her and replied with "Yes." Her next move was to send me to the office for disciplinary attention. Fortunately the principal took time to ask what had happened. He recognized the difference between ignorance of social norms and insolence. After drying my tears, he explained that I was to always remember to say "Yes, Ma'am," "No, Ma'am," "Yes, Sir," or "No, Sir." This was very hard for me to do. Where I had started school, saying "ma'am" and "sir" would have been considered rude. He let me practice with him before sending me back to Mrs. Horn. She and I got along just fine after that.

How can a teacher minimize confusion and efficiently establish classroom limits?

1. Separate rules and expectations from routines and procedures (Alberto & Troutman, 1990; Sprick & Howard, 1997). Expectations are the broadly stated values by which a group agrees to work and live together. Rules are specifically stated behavioral standards. Routines and procedures address the mundane organizational components of classroom management such as how and when to submit completed work, when to sharpen pencils, how to access permission to use the restroom, etc.

2. Clearly define expectations, rules, and routines or procedures (Alberto & Troutman, 1990; Sprick & Howard, 1997). Examples of each of those components of an effective classroom plan are included in the Appendix.

3. Develop a list of behaviors with the students that represent the values stated in the expectations (Sprick, Sprick, & Garrison, 1992; Lewis & Sugai, 1999). Respect, for example, might be defined as behaviors that help people feel comfortable in the classroom. Students could then generate a list of respectful behaviors such as (a) asking before using someone else's materials, (b) using an inside voice, (c) taking turns when using classroom equipment, and (d) taking turns when talking. A graphic organizer and suggested lesson plan for developing expectations with students is provided in Appendix A.

4. Rules should be limited to non-negotiable absolute standards for behavior. Select rules that are few in number, positively stated, and are descriptive of observable behavior (Alberto & Troutman, 1990). Avoid rules such as "Do your best." or "Be kind." Those are expectations. Rules should be so clear that anyone would be able to understand them without further explanation. Examples of effective rules include (a) Keep hands, feet, and other objects to yourself; (b) Complete tasks on time; and (c) Remain in your assigned area. A rule that states that tasks will be completed on time avoids issues over art activities or game time. Regardless of the activity—academic or social—the rule addresses timely completion.

5. Identify common routines and procedures that are necessary for smooth transitions (Sprick, Sprick, & Garrison, 1992) Students need to know what to do when entering the classroom in the morning, how to line up for lunch, and what to do at the end of the day when preparing to go home. Children benefit tremendously from having clearly stated routines and procedures, practicing them regularly, and reviewing them as needed.

6. Avoid the temptation to open non-negotiable items for class discussion.

7. Illustrate the expectations, rules, and routines or procedures to enhance the understanding of students with reading or language processing problems.

8. Re-teach rules, procedures, routines, and expectations prior to and after holidays, when new students arrive, and when a substitute is called (Lewis & Sugai, 1999). Plans for reviewing expectations, rules, and procedures can be included in the substitute folder. A game for that purpose is included in Appendix G.

Early in the development of the class at KDJ Elementary, the guidance counselor, Ms. Gentry, attempted to establish expectations and rules with the students for use during guidance lessons. Her experience with the students serves as a nonexample for many of the items listed in the recommendations above.

Ms. Gentry sat on the floor, spread markers and poster board in front of her, and said,

"O.K., boys and girls, let's get to know each other a little better. Please tell me your names and anything else you'd like for me to know."

Ms. Gentry had requested that a teacher be present but not actively involved. I sat in the back of the room and observed. The students fidgeted for a few moments before Tomika began.

"I'm Tomika. I'm 8 years old." The boys took turns identifying themselves and waited for Ms. Gentry's next direction.

"Well, it is very nice to meet you. We will be working together every Thursday morning. Today, I would like for you to help me make some rules for us to follow during our time together."

"What do you mean?" Tomika asked suspiciously.

"That's a good question, Tomika. I would like for us to agree on rules for behavior."

Tomika rolled her eyes. The boys began to snicker.

Marcos stood up and announced that the first rule should be that everyone could say whatever he wanted.

"Do you really think that would be best?"

"Yeah, we could cuss at each other."

Lydel jumped up to demonstrate. "Yeh, Marcos! You're such a dumb ass, we'll have a great time ripping on you."

Under typical circumstances, Marcos would not have allowed anyone to speak to him in that manner. The amused smiles on the faces of all the students signaled the game they had devised at the expense of Ms. Gentry. Marcos countered with, "You better watch your mouth, man. You keep it up and I'll kick you so hard in your butt that you shit tennis shoes for a week!"

The rest of the group was rolling on the floor in laughter at this point.

Ms. Gentry continued. "Now, boys, do you really think that this would help us work together? I'm sure we could come up with some rules that would encourage us to share our feelings without being rude or disrespectful to each other."

Lydel started to say something when Marcos cut him off. "Look, bitch. We know what you want us to say. You know what you want us to say. So, just cut the crap and tell us the rules."

Ms. Gentry meant well. In many classrooms teachers engage students in a discussion about the rules as a method for building a sense of shared ownership in the group processes and responsibility for personal behavior. Some students, however, respond to open-ended discussions of this type with less-than-desirable results. Non-negotiable rules should be stated clearly by the teacher. Rules related to limits on verbal and physical aggression can and should be clarified and enforced. People are not for hurting. Any attempt on the part of the children to attack the teacher or each other physically must be disallowed from the beginning and stopped immediately if the behavior occurs.

Expectations can be developed together as a group once basic rules are discussed and taught. After Ms. Gentry and I engaged in some problemsolving, the guidance lesson proceeded as described below the following week.

ANECDOTE

Prior to Ms. Gentry's arrival, I asked the students to arrange their desks in a semi-circle. I placed a rocking chair, easel, and markers at the opening of the semi-circle before directing students to be seated in their desks. Ms Gentry entered carrying poster boards and an art caddy with student scissors, glue, and discarded magazines of various types.

"Good morning, boys and girls."

An unenthusiastic "Hi" arose in unison from the group. They could tell from the arrangement of the furniture that they would not be rolling on the floor or yelling profanity at each other this time.

"Before we begin our lesson on expectations, I want to share a few rules with you." Ms. Gentry displayed a large poster with brightly illustrated pictures and boldly printed captions.

The first picture was of students seated in their desks. Underneath the picture was printed in large letters "Remain in your assigned area." The next picture was of students working in pairs with art materials. The rule underneath this picture was "Keep hands, feet, and other objects to yourself." The third picture was of a student working on an assignment. The rule for that picture was "Complete tasks on time." The fourth picture on the poster was of two students playing a game. The caption read "Use kind, school-appropriate words." The last picture on the poster was of a child raising his hand. The rule for that picture was "Talk when it is your turn."

Ms. Gentry took time to discuss each rule with the students. They conducted individual and group role plays to practice applying the rules. After that, she gave the students paper plate faces with a smile on one side and a frown on the other side. As she showed them pictures of students who were following the rules and pictures of students who were not following the rules, she asked the students to hold up the paper plate picture that represented how the students were performing. A happy face meant that the students in the picture were following the rule. A sad face meant that the students in the picture were not following the rule. Tomika and the boys loved the role plays and the paper plate game. Ms. Gentry praised them for their insight and accuracy. This review of the rules took only 10 minutes and set limits on behavior that had previously spun out of control.

With rules clearly understood and practiced, the group was ready to begin the process of selecting expectations that they could all agree to live by. Expectations are value statements. The skills necessary for full mastery of an expectation may gradually increase as students' abilities allow. This group decided that everyone should be honest, kind, and helpful. They took time to define each word by describing behaviors that represent those values.

Honesty was described as (a) telling the truth, (b) asking before touching something that belongs to another person, and (c) doing your own work. Kindness included (a) giving compliments, (b) not saying mean names or put-downs, and (c) taking turns. The group agreed that helpful people (a) clean up their messes; (b) offer to do things for others such as hold a door, carry books, or get supplies; and (c) ask questions before getting mad. The students illustrated these expectations and wrote the behaviors under the illustrated posters to help everyone remember how to demonstrate honesty, kindness, and helpfulness. All staff members who worked with these students also agreed to live by the expectations. Rules are non-negotiable and absolute. Rules provide the structure that children who have inadequate levels of self-control need during the initial stages of group development. Rules also provide structure for well-functioning groups. Expectations, on the other hand, describe the desired climate or culture of the classroom. Expectations are supportive of all members of the group and can enhance the group's cohesiveness.

Students with emotional and behavioral disorders sometimes hit or kick first and talk about the problem later. Each teacher should have a rule prohibiting physical aggression and guidelines for handling aggression if it occurs. There are programs that teach intervention strategies aimed at de-escalating situations appropriately using physical proximity, redirecting attention, and intervening verbally. A teacher can do a great deal to prevent physical aggression by creatively arranging classroom supplies and furniture, remaining calm in spite of upsetting behavior, and being alert for signs of trouble.

General guidelines to follow when establishing limits include the following:

1. Keep rules to a minimum (Alberto & Troutman, 1990).

2. State rules clearly (Alberto & Troutman, 1990). In some cases, "stay in your area" may mean having a square taped to the floor around the desk. Putting one toe over the line would mean being out of your area.

3. Provide students with a hierarchy of consequences, both positive and negative. Compliance means rewards. Noncompliance means punishments (Alberto & Troutman, 1990).

4. Be as good as your word. If three talk-outs in 15 minutes earns 3 minutes in a cool-off chair, then stick to it. Don't get mad and send the student to the chair after two talk-outs. Don't let six go by before responding (Alberto & Troutman, 1990).

5. Don't promise rewards or punishments that are not possible (Alberto & Troutman, 1990).

6. Only demand behavior that can be enforced (Alberto & Troutman, 1990). Be specific about what students must accomplish. Telling a student that a special activity will be earned if he or she has been "on task" only invites arguments. The student will inevitably claim that he or she was "trying" to finish.

7. Model the appropriate response for the children at every opportunity. Discuss your behavior as well as the students' positive steps toward self-control at regular times each day. This technique works slowly over time. While it does not produce instant, measurable changes in behavior, it is a powerful tool of instruction when used consistently (Driekurs, Grumwald, & Pepper, 1982; Glasser, 1998).

8. As closely as possible, have the punishment fit the crime (Alberto & Troutman, 1990). Sitting in a chair in the corner for being off task doesn't make as much sense as missing all or part of a special activity while completing the task. Teaching students that their behavior is under their control and that consequences are more often than not a result of their own behavior is the toughest part of the educational process. A student who completes the work on time can be told, "You have chosen to get your work done even though you felt like quitting. Now you have time for a special activity. Aren't you glad that you decided to use your time wisely today?"

9. Keep power struggles to a minimum. Set limits by using impersonal, measurable criteria (Alberto & Troutman, 1990). Timers that "ding" to signal the end of an activity, for example, are easier for some children to respond to than the teacher's telling them to stop. It is also helpful to post schedules, daily independent work assignments, and lists of rules and consequences on walls and bulletin boards for students to refer to.

10. Be positive. Setting limits is healthy. It does not have to be done in a rude or hostile way. Firmness does not mean intimidation.

11. Set limits by requesting behavior that is incompatible with the undesirable behavior (Alberto & Troutman, 1990). Many times it will be far more effective to say "Hands at your sides!" instead of "Don't hit!"

12. Give students choices (Glasser, 1998). The fact that they have choices should be a constant topic of each conversation concerning behavior. An example might be "I see that this assignment is taking longer than you had hoped. You may choose to finish it now or you may use part of your lunch period to complete it. The work must be done by the end of lunch if you plan to attend the special activity period. You may decide when you want to finish the assignment."

13. Use physical proximity to help students correct their own behavior (Redl, 1966). Moving closer to a student who is off task, talking, or showing signs of agitation often results in compliance without a word being said directly to the student.

14. Redirect attention to get students out of stressful situations before they lose composure (Redl's (1966) "antiseptic bouncing"). Select students who are acting appropriately to go on errands or do jobs. Stapling papers, filing, collating worksheet packets, and cleaning chalkboard erasers are common favorites. This strategy can divert a child's attention, prevent a fight, and give the teacher time to deal with students who are acting inappropriately and/or instigating misbehavior. Other situations to which this technique applies include academic stress relief and helping overactive children find acceptable uses for their energy.

The following anecdote illustrates several useful techniques.

ANECDOTE

"Kevin, you need a class behind you if you want to be a leader."

"I am the leader! It's my day."

"I know, Kevin. But, if you get too far ahead, you'll be walking alone."

"OK, I'll slow down."

"Thank you, Kevin. That's just the right speed. I see Jonathan, Lydel, Tommy, and Tomika walking quietly with hands at their sides. Nice walking, people!"

As the students file into the room and settle quietly into their seats, I keep my eyes and ears open for subtle signs of moods and needs. Away from the crowds at the bus area, Lydel is calmer and tries to help Tommy with his booksack.

"Hey, man, I can get that buckle undone for you."

"Leave me alone," Tommy whines.

"What's your problem? I just wanted to help."

"Lydel, I think Tommy's still unhappy about what happened at the bus."

"Yeah! I'm not a baby! And, I don't need your help."

"Oh! OK. Be that way. See if I care!"

"Lydel, thank you for wanting to help. Let Tommy take care of his own booksack. I think he can handle it. Would you like to help Ms. Agnew file homework papers?"

"Sure!"

I walk from desk to desk collecting homework, putting play money into banks, and talking positively to each student.

"Kevin, you did your math and spelling homework and led our line at just the right speed. You also earned your bus points. And now I see that you are ready for class. You've earned 25 cents already this morning, and you've only been here 5 minutes!" Kevin smiles and sits up straight as I go to the next desk.

"Tomika, I like your neat handwriting on this spelling homework. But where is your math?"

"I forgot it."

"Bring it back tomorrow, and you can still get credit for it. OK?"

"OK."

"And thank you for talking nicely to Tommy on the bus. It really helps. You've earned 15 cents."

"How's it going, Tommy?" No response. . . . "Tommy, it's OK. I know you were upset earlier. But, I'm not mad." No response.... "If you have your homework, I need to see it. Otherwise, you won't get paid."

"Come on, Tommy. Give her your homework. You know you want to go to the classroom store today." Tomika urges him gently.

Slowly, Tommy's head rises, and two crumpled papers unfold in his open hands.

"Thank you, Tommy. I know it's hard to talk when you're upset. Sitting quietly right now is a good decision. Turning In your homework and walking to the classroom on your own were also good decisions. Here is your money for homework and appropriate line behavior."

"What about my money for bus behavior?"

"I'm sorry, Tommy. You decided to act inappropriately on the bus. You did not earn your money or points for that."

Tommy's head goes down again as I pat his shoulder and move on.

"Well, look at Marcus! The bus driver tells me that you were quiet and appropriate this morning."

"So?"

"So, I'm pleased."

"Wow! You're pleased. Everybody clap. Mrs. Rockwell is p-l-e-a-s-e-d." Marcus has difficulty accepting compliments. The class can easily be disrupted by disrespectful comments if tension is really high. When the class is able to ignore inappropriate remarks, however, it is helpful to focus on the positive and ignore discounting statements.

"Thank you for earning your bus points and money, Marcus."

"All right, Jonathan! Mrs. Crenshaw will be so proud of the work you put into this math homework!"

"Do you think I can start going to Mrs. Crenshaw's class for science, too?"

"That depends on you, Jonathan. How do you earn that privilege?"

"Earn my points and do my work."

"Right!"

"Lydel, are you ready to be paid?"

"Where do you need to be first?"

"In my seat."

"OK. There you go. Thank you for helping Ms. Agnew."

All of this takes less than 5 minutes. Starting the day out positively puts money in the bank in more ways than one. As the teacher, I am responsible for doing everything in my power to set a cooperative tone for the day.

Avoid fights by redirecting attention and energy. Avoid power struggles by making it clear that each person makes his or her own decisions. Ignore disrespectful comments meant to discount earned rewards. Face each day with a firm belief in each student's desire and ability to grow. These are all unspoken messages behind the teacher's words and actions.

SAFETY

Safety is the number one priority in a classroom for children with behavior problems. Poor impulse control, low tolerance for frustration, physical aggressiveness, and limited contact with reality make for potentially hazardous conditions. Careful attention to the physical environment of the classroom is the first line of defense in preventing problems.

General guidelines for room arrangement include the following:

1. Provide students with adequate space around their desks. If students are seated so that they can touch each other easily without getting up, stealing and hitting problems could escalate.

2. Keep all items not in immediate use in cabinets or closets. Lock the cabinets or closets if possible. The more items available for an angry child to throw, the more rewarding and potentially harmful the tantrum becomes.

3. Keep scissors, box cutters, and other potential weapons out of students' reach.

4. Closely supervise art and cooking activities. Make it clear that these activities will stop if rules are not followed.

5. If necessary, arrange furniture to provide students with visual barriers during independent work times.

6. Make areas of the room activity specific. For example, desks are for work; the rug is for play; the large table is for group discussion; and the time-out corner is for cooling off and thinking. This helps the students develop constructive classroom behavior habits and reduces confusion over what behavior is expected at a given place and time.

7. Check activity-specific areas for appropriate space, lighting, storage, and furniture needs.

8. Remove everything from the room that is not absolutely necessary.

9. Make furniture and materials accessible to students in order to increase productivity and decrease anger and frustration.

10. Actively enforce the rule that people are not for hurting. Providing children with a sense of psychological safety is included in the section on trust. The following anecdote, however, provides a vivid picture of how important a sense of safety is to these students.

ANECDOTE

"OK. Quickly now, group! What are our class rules?"

Kevin yells, "No fighting."

I ignore him and, without looking at anyone, I raise my hand. As Kevin gets the hint and raises his own hand, I call on him. "Kevin, thank you for raising your hand."

"No fighting."

"That's true, Kevin. We don't want fighting in here. But our rules tell us what we do want. What rule tells us the appropriate behavior?"

"Keep hands, feet, and other objects to yourself."

"All right, Kevin. Here's your penny for a correct answer. Anyone else?" Tomika's hand shoots up as she sees the play money being handed out. "Yes, Tomika?"

"Raise your hand and wait to be called on."

"Terrific!" I flip a penny into her bank. We're on a roll.

From the review of classroom rules, we move quickly to a question-and-answer session on calendar skills. My aide, Ms. Agnew, is usually busy getting attendance, breakfast and lunch money, and homework papers sorted. The brief 10-to-15 minute question-and-

answer session before breakfast helps orient the children each morning.

In spite of average or better IQs, these children frequently lack the most basic information about days, months, and seasons. Daily, structured drills on naming, recognizing, ordering, and classifying such information using word and picture card cues works better than a concentrated unit taught over a shorter period of time.

"You all are going to break my bank! With so many correct answers I'm almost out of pennies. Who would like to trade 5 pennies for a nickel?"

"Thank you for raising your hand, Tommy. Here you are."

"There you go, Tomika."

"Thank you, Marcus."

"All right, Lydel, Kevin, and Jonathan."

"OK, as I call your name, you may go one at a time to be seated at the big table in the cooking area. Ms. Agnew has breakfast ready for you. Remember to select a chair and stay in that chair. Getting up to change seats will result in having to come back to your desk. Kevin, you're our leader today, so you may go first."

Kevin moves quickly to the table and takes a seat after washing his hands.

"Tomika, you may go now. I really like the way you have been sitting quietly and remembering to raise your hand."

Out of the corner of my eye I see Lydel getting up. As I turn toward him, I see that his eyes are glazed. He is heading for Marcus, but I step between them. "Lydel, please sit down."

"Get away, bitch. You ain't no teacher to me. Move or I'll. . ."

"Lydel, you have until the count of three to be in your seat. One.., two..."

As I start to count, he turns toward his desk. My room has no call button. I rarely need to call for the principal; but when I do, I must send a student or my aide. Lydel has learned from past experiences with me that I do not allow people to hurt each other, themselves, or me if I can stop it. He knows I only restrain as a last resort, but that I will do it as a safety measure.

By the time I get to three, he is sitting in his desk. His fists are clenched and his face is tense and angry, but his eyes are clearer now.

"I can see that your muscles are tight. I appreciate your decision to sit instead of doing something inappropriate. That was a good choice!"

"Tommy, you can wash your hands and sit at the big table now. Jonathan, when Tommy is finished, you have permission to get up."

I let Ms. Agnew supervise breakfast while I turn my attention to Marcus and Lydel.

Lydel has voices that tell him when someone is going to hurt him. The voices have absolutely nothing to do with what is really happening in the room at the time. But Marcus likes to stick his middle finger up at people in inconspicuous ways to get a reaction from his peers. When these two are involved, I'm never sure how it all really started until we talk.

Once a fight actually occurs, it makes no difference who started it. Both students receive the same consequence if neither student attempted to stop the fight, but knowing how a problem started is helpful in planning avoidance strategies. That is why we talk.

It turns out this time that Lydel heard voices. Lydel tells me that his "protection" told him to beat up Marcus.

Marcus is rewarded with bonus points for staying quiet and seated. Letting an adult handle such a situation is a giant step forward for him. Lydel is told that voice or no voice, fighting is out. The decision to sit on the count of "three" was excellent. Because of that decision, no time out is necessary. But he does earn zeros on his point card for that time period. I make a note to myself to call Lydel's aunt and the mental health clinic about his medication.

As Marcus and Lydel join the others, breakfast is under way.

The section that follows addresses trust and psychological safety. All of these components are so vitally interrelated that it is difficult to separate them even for discussion. It is crucial for adults who work with these children to understand the importance of each component from the point of view of the child.

TRUST

Trust and psychological safety are inseparable. In order for a child to learn effectively as a member of a classroom group, a sense of trust and safety in self and others must be established.

Because children with behavior problems are often low on impulse control, a highly structured, predictable routine is a prerequisite to their developing a sense of trust.

A daily schedule is a good technique for behavior management. When establishing a schedule with a new group, adjustments may be needed during the first month. Each group has its own rhythm and personality. A balance between whole group instruction and independent study must be made based on the group's abilities and needs. Once a schedule is established, however, make every effort to follow it. Students develop a sense of trust in the teacher and in themselves when their daily routines are predictable.

When a balanced, predictable schedule is established in conjunction with a clearly defined, consistently executed behavior management system, students begin building trust.

Following are some suggestions for establishing trust in the classroom:

1. Be as good as your word. If a treat, punishment, special activity, or assignment under the teacher's control is promised, follow through. Children with behavior problems distrust even the best excuse a teacher gives.

2. Do not use intimidating actions or statements as a form of behavior control. While young children may respond out of fear, the price of such intimidation is high. The message teachers send by using intimidation tactics is that it's OK to frighten smaller, less physically capable people into submission. Older students are more apt to become physically aggressive toward a threatening adult.

3. Deal with noncompliant behavior consistently.

4. Make sure rewards and punishments relate logically to the student's actions.

5. Use punishment as a tool of instruction rather than revenge.

6. Be honest with students.

7. Prepare students in advance for any changes. Substitute teachers, visitors, new classmates, schedule changes, fire drills, and even holiday vacations can catch students by surprise and cause an escalation of negative behavior. Talking about such events ahead of time and having a plan for dealing with them increases students' sense of self-control and trust.

8. As the students are ready, enlist them in some of the decision-making in the classroom. If a weekly art or cooking activity is part of the schedule, allow the students to choose which activity they want to do. Giving them increasing opportunities to make appropriate choices increases their sense of trust, control, and positive regard for the rights of others.

9. Use language that conveys acceptance and trust. Have students describe what they can do. De-emphasize what they cannot do.

10. Structure academic assignments for success. Students know when they are working below their ability level. Real feelings of accomplishment will not develop if lessons are too easy. Moving too quickly may be discouraging. Encourage skill mastery by structuring the introduction of new concepts in small, digestible chunks. For example, when introducing equivalent fractions, use different colored construction paper strips first. For a day or two, have students "play" with the strips to find out how many pinks equal a blue, and so forth. Color names are easier to talk about at first. After the students are comfortable with the concept, introduce the math words: "Two pinks equal one blue, or two fourths equal one half."

In every subject area, use manipulative materials, art, and music to help students bridge the gaps between concrete and abstract concepts. In science, use experiments and models. In math, use manipulatives. In social studies, use models, 3-D maps and globes, art, and music. In reading and language, use charts, models, art, and music. Active participation not only improves academic achievement, but also captures students' interests, thereby preventing behavior problems that occur due to frustration, boredom, or dislike of an assignment.

11. Review the day's events each morning before beginning academic lessons. If a substitute will be handling a class one day, discuss this with the students and prepare them for the change. If an assembly or some other event will alter the usual math or reading time, explain that. Even older students will resist changes if they come as a surprise. A little grumbling first thing in the morning is easier to deal with than a blowup later.

Elements of the process of establishing trust are highlighted as the anecdotal illustration continues to unfold.

ANECDOTE

"OK, people, this is how the day looks. We will have our usual morning schedule. Recess, for those who have earned it, will begin at the second bell."

"Who remembers what special class we have on Tuesdays? Tomika?"

"Music."

"Right. And who is the music teacher? Tommy?"

"Um... um... Mrs. Smythe?"

"You remembered! Thank you, Tommy. We will go to music at our usual time today. When we get back to the room, we will have classroom store. Keep that in mind as you answer questions, complete assignments, and walk in line. Every little bit adds up."

Breakfast and academic periods run smoothly this morning, but I begin to sense a triangle of tension brewing among Kevin, Marcus, and Jonathan. I know Kevin is jealous of Jonathan's mainstreaming success. Kevin has been with me longer and feels that he is entitled to more privileges even if his behavior does not consistently warrant it. Jonathan's growing sense of self-respect no longer allows insults to collapse his resolve. I silently applaud his decision to stand up for himself, but I am also aware of my responsibility to help Jonathan learn acceptable ways of asserting himself.

As the second bell rings, Ms. Agnew and I call the students to the line one at a time.

Everyone has earned a 15-minute break by completing assignments and acting appropriately. Our little group is the only one on the playground at this time.

Having recess with the rest of the school would be too overwhelming for the class.

Ms. Agnew and I chat as the children climb the monkey bars, run, and roll in the grass. Recess is usually a relaxing time for all of us.

I have a message from the office to take a phone call. Normally, I don't leave a whole group alone with my aide; but I know that Ms. Dodd, the social worker, is on her way, so I leave. The call is from the special education office. We will be getting a new student next week.

As I turn down the sidewalk to our recess area after taking the call in the office, Kevin runs at top speed toward me, holding his eye and screaming.

"My eye! My eye! Where were you, bitch? Get away. You ain't no teacher to me. This wouldn't have happened if you were out there. Oh... Oh..,."

By this time, Kevin is on his back, rolling from side to side, kicking his feet, and holding his left eye. Each attempt to check the severity of his injury is met with another round of insults. I finally convince Kevin to walk back to the classroom with me. Ms. Dodd, Ms. Agnew, and the rest of the class are waiting outside the students' restroom. Jonathan's fair-skinned face is flushed, and sweat is dripping from his hairline. He will not make eye contact, and his fists are clenched, indicating that he was involved.

Marcus has his back to all of us, arms crossed against his muscular chest, and foot tapping furiously.

Tomika, Lydel, and Tommy show varying degrees of either amusement or disinterest.

I ask Ms. Dodd to get Kevin some ice and help Ms. Agnew with our usual story time.

Kevin, Jonathan, Marcus, and I have some serious problem-solving to do.

Before I begin talking about the incident with the boys, Ms. Agnew tells me that she hadn't noticed anything happening until she heard Jonathan screaming. From what she could see, Kevin had been making fun of Jonathan. Jonathan screamed at Kevin to shut up and threatened to punch him if he didn't. Kevin kept it up and laughed. Before Ms. Agnew could get to them, Marcus, who had been watching from a few yards away, took a running start and plowed full force into Kevin. Kevin was so startled by Marcus's surprise attack that he didn't have time to react before Marcus had punched him in the eye, jumped up, and taken off toward the fence.

By this time, Ms. Dodd had arrived. She went to talk Marcus out of climbing over the fence and running away. Ms. Agnew tried to comfort Kevin, but when she saw that he was determined to find me, she let him go and turned her attention to the other students.

All of this happened within a few short minutes.

Armed with the facts, I am ready to problem solve with each boy and plan ahead for the group. Teaching these boys to accept each other is a priority.

ACCEPTANCE

It is important to accept children's differing abilities, temperaments, and personal strengths and weaknesses. In addition, acceptance of the limitations of the environment; co-workers; county, state, and federal guidelines; available resources; and the number of hours in a day means informed, healthy recognition. Acceptance is not to be confused with blind compliance, approval, or resignation.

To the students, a teacher's acceptance of them means that he or she continues to be fair, consistent, and professional even when they have tested his or her tolerance unmercifully. To co-workers, acceptance means a willingness to provide mutual support. To supervisors, acceptance means getting all of the paperwork done on time in spite of its monotony. With regard to the environment and available resources, acceptance means creative utilization of everyone and everything possible.

To the individual teacher, acceptance means being aware of personal strengths and weaknesses. Take time out to rest, relax, and learn. Teaching requires a great deal of mental and emotional stamina. Be alert to signs of personal stress. Take the signs seriously. As a Master's project during one of my graduate courses, I investigated teacher's methods of coping with the stress of teaching students with severe emotional and behavioral disorders. Teachers from three schools reported that early in their careers they had resorted to eating comfort foods which caused many of them to gain unwanted pounds. Over time, they began to use humor, exercise, and talks with loved ones or colleagues as a way to deal with the stress. I have a particularly strong ability to visualize images in response to words that I hear and sometimes have to suppress the urge to laugh when students begin to vent their anger. When one student referred to another staff member as an "a_ _ hole in the middle," for example, I immediately visualized a bare behind and wondered just where the student imagined the anus to be. That was not the time for asking questions about the student's knowledge of anatomy, of course, but tucking that anecdote away for future reflection does add some humor into an otherwise tiresome exchange. Additional suggestions for avoiding the negative effects of stress related to teaching students with challenging behaviors are provided in Chapter 8.

In the classroom, acceptance of the students by the teacher leads to acceptance by the students of each other and themselves. Positive, observable ways to convey acceptance are included in the following list:

1. Provide bulletin board space in the room with each child's name on it for the display of artwork and academic papers.

2. Distribute notes to the children describing positive behavior you have noticed during the day, week, or month.

3. Make occasional phone calls or home visits to parents to discuss positive behavior.

4. Use words to describe unacceptable behavior. Refrain from using words that attack the child's sense of self-worth. For example you might say, "I do not like it when I see you kicking the chair. Tell me how you feel with words." This statement reflects respect for the child while describing the undesirable behavior. An ineffective statement might be, "Quit acting like a baby. I'm sick of having you disrupt this class."

5. Recognize students with a card, cake, or special activity on their birthdays.

6. Have a regularly scheduled time each day or week to discuss positive things the students have noticed about each other. In the beginning, model and define the appropriate responses. Structure the discussion around a specific theme such as academic strengths, work habits, or talents.

7. When a class is having difficulty accepting other classmates due to their inappropriate behavior, give them time to vent their feelings in an appropriate way by having them list specific behaviors they dislike. Respect their right to feel the way they do. Then enlist their cooperation in helping the ostracized student or students become part of the group. Rewarding the class for responding appropriately to the student who is acting inappropriately, along with repeating the discussion process as needed, strengthens the class's tolerance for disruptive behavior. They quickly learn to remain in control in spite of another's actions. Problems do not escalate as quickly, are resolved more efficiently, and take less time away from instruction.

8. Admit your own mistakes or limitations. Not everyone is an expert at everything. "I don't know," "Let's find out together," or "I'm sorry I snapped at you a moment ago" are phrases that show self-acceptance. Modeling self-acceptance is one way of teaching it to the students.

9. Mistakes are a valuable part of the learning process. Teach students to accept mistakes as a way of gaining information rather than as proof of their decreased value as human beings. Use nonthreatening activities such as jigsaw puzzles, pencil and paper mazes, and games that use clues to illustrate that through trial and error, correct responses can be learned. Relate this to other social and academic situations.

10. Ask students to talk positively about themselves at least once a day using sentence starters that emphasize behaviors and achievements that are under their control.

Examples include:

I handled _____ well today.

I learned _____ today.
I improved at _____ today.
I feel great when I _____.
I have a talent for _____.
I'm a good friend because _____.
My best subject is _____.
People like the way I _____.

Remaining aware of the power of acceptance during the stresses involved in managing a class of children with behavior problems is difficult. The following anecdotal section reflects many of the techniques discussed in this section.

ANECDOTE

Tomika spins around to face me. Her body is tense as she begins to talk.

"I'm not going. I hate her! She's mean and ugly. I'm not going, and you can't make me!"

I walk closer to Tomika's desk and kneel in front of it.

"Tomika, no one is going to try to make you go. The decision is yours. I know you hate Ms. Smythe. She touches you when you don't want her to. It's OK not to like someone. If you decide not to go, you can stay here with Ms. Agnew. You will not earn points, because you will not be in your assigned area. But you will earn work sign-offs if you complete work while the class is at music. If you go with us, I promise to stay right by your side to help you. You will earn points, and you will earn an extra quarter to use in the classroom store if you are appropriate with Ms. Smythe. It's up to you, Tomika."

Tomika squirms a little in her chair. Having a good point card is important to her. Earning money for our classroom store is also very reinforcing. Tears fill her eyes.

She hasn't seen Ms. Smythe since the last time she tried to strangle her.

"OK, I'll go. Where's the quarter?"

"Right here. I'll keep it in my hand the whole time we're there so you can see it."

"Will you promise to sit right with me?"

"Tomika, I won't leave your side. If it looks like things are getting too hard, we'll leave. OK?"

"OK," Tomika replies in a small, timid voice very unlike her usual loud, aggressive front. The class senses Tomika's tension and is quieter than usual on the walk to Ms. Smythe's room. We manage to get seated before she arrives. As she walks into the room, Tomika grabs my hand and holds on for dear life.

"You! . . . Yes, you over there!" Ms. Smythe is shaking her finger at a boy who usually acts silly during her lessons but is sitting quietly at the moment. "I just want you to know right now, young man, that I won't be putting up with your foolishness today." Ms. Smythe's speech goes

on for a few more minutes, detailing sins of the past. So much for positive reinforcement. A once-calm classroom is gearing up for the very trouble Ms. Smythe is predicting.

When Ms. Smythe spots Tomika, I become wary. I have second thoughts about putting Tomika through so much this soon. Ms. Smythe walks straight back to where Tomika and I are sitting. Here we go—ready or not.

"Hello, Tomika," Ms. Smythe begins in a sweet, high-pitched voice. "Do you remember me?"

Tomika does her best to become one with the chair she is sitting in as she nods, "Yes" without making eye contact.

I can see how tense, angry, and panicked Tomika is. When she looks at me, I smile a little, show her the quarter and whisper, "You're doing great."

Ms. Smythe can't leave it at that. She seems determined to bring out the worst in Tomika.

"Well, dear, I'm so glad that you're here." Her words do not match her tone. "And look at the adorable little dress you have on." Ms. Smythe starts lifting the skirt hem slightly, patting Tomika's knee and touching her sleeves.

Tomika makes a few small squeaks. Every muscle in her body looks ready to explode. But she holds on. With all her might, she works to control the urge to lash out violently.

I, too, feel angry and have my own impulses with which to contend. Ms. Smythe and I have discussed Tomika privately. I have explained Tomika's need for taking things slowly. Why must she goad the child into a problem? So many of the other teachers are willing to learn ways of helping.

Ms. Smythe looks at me in amazement. The test is over. Tomika has neither cursed nor attacked Ms. Smythe. As Ms. Smythe goes on with her lesson, I whisper to Tomika about how proud I am of her. She has made excellent decisions. She has shown appropriate behavior in spite of extreme anger. I wanted to hug her.

Within 3 months, Tomika is volunteering to help Ms. Smythe as well as initiating contact with hugs and asking to hold her hand as they walk. I have never dreamed things would go so well. Yeah, Tomika!

The elements of limit setting, safety, trust, and acceptance create an environment that is safe physically and emotionally. Once that is accomplished, children are capable of benefiting from instruction.

SENSE OF PURPOSE

A sense of purpose can go a long way in helping groups build on positive, constructive activities and avoid time-consuming problems. Students bring many negatively charged preconceptions about themselves, teachers, and schools into the room. Letting students know from the beginning that the classroom is a place to learn, that there is a job to do, and that appropriate participation in learning activities is expected saves time. Many of the "I can't," "Make me," and "Forget you" reactions can be avoided with careful attention to details.

The following techniques can be adapted to provide a sense of purpose to both younger and older students:

1. Tape work sign-off sheets to students' desks, folders, or bulletin board areas. Preferred activities during the day or week are contingent upon completion of work. The sign-off sheet can be used as a record of completed assignments. The teacher or aide can put one initial for completion of half of an assignment and both initials for completing a full assignment.

2. Structure lessons as closely as possible to resemble those in regular education classes. Weekly spelling tests are one example of activities that students in regular classes are required to perform. Word lists can be selected with success in mind by limiting the number or type of words chosen each week.

3. Grade papers and record the grades. Expect corrections to be made if work is incorrect. Special activities cannot be earned if work is not corrected.

4. Keep an ongoing, whole group project of some kind in progress at all times. Building a model town for social studies, typing a student newspaper for language arts, producing a "rap" tape, or constructing science models are just a few ways to keep academics alive while providing a social activity for focusing energy and enthusiasm. Protect group projects when the class is not working on them. Lock them in a cabinet or closet. Otherwise, an angry child might attempt to destroy all or part of the group project, setting off a chain reaction in the whole group.

5. Help students set realistic academic goals. Keep charts of their progress. A bulletin board or special folder can be used to display the progress charts. Keep positive evidence of the students' abilities to learn posted for times when motivation or self-esteem needs an honest boost.

A sense of purpose can keep the class moving in the right direction during academic instruction as well as during times of transition. The following anecdotal section illustrates how a group's sense of purpose helps the group prepare for a new student. Aspects of limit setting, safety, trust, and acceptance are also evident.

ANECDOTE

By the afternoon, Ms. Dodd has gathered more information about our newest arrival. In 2 days, 8-year-old Jason will be joining our group. Physical aggression, profanity, and a lack of respect for authority in such a young child are hard to understand.

Ms. Dodd asks, "Are you sure you want this one?"

"Yes, I'm ready. I'll just wear my boots and eat my Wheaties."

Preparing the class for a newcomer is my first job. The class helps me get a desk, bulletin board space, point chart, and other materials ready for him. We talk while we do this.

"How old is he?"

"Does he like to fight?"

"Is he black or white?"

"Does he like to fight?"

"Is he smart or retarded?"

"Does he like to fight?"

"Is he strong?"

"Does he like to fight?"

"Will you still help us or will you just help him 'cause he's new?"

"Does he like to fight?"

"Will he have to earn his points to cook, too?"

"Does he like to fight?"

On and on, the questions never seem to end. A new student means a new power hierarchy within the group. They'll be watching me and each other for every slight sign of real or imagined favoritism or antagonism. Fighting is this group's favorite way of settling things, so questions about fighting continue to dominate our conversations. As our efforts to provide Jason with a comfortable welcome are completed, I gather the group for our final discussion before Jason's arrival the next morning.

"You have done a terrific job of getting things ready for Jason. Tomika and Tommy have decorated a welcome banner. Marcus helped get his desk in order and put tape on the floor around it. Jonathan and Lydel fixed a bulletin board display area for his work. And Kevin helped Ms. Agnew run off charts and worksheets for him. You have each earned extra bonus points and a treat for working so nicely together. Thank you! Now, one last time. How can we help Jason tomorrow? Kevin?"

"Say hello. Don't laugh or say inappropriate things to him."

"OK, I like that, Kevin."

"Tomika?"

"If he says something to us we don't like, ignore him."

Marcus jumps up with, "Not me! I'll knock him out if he bothers me."

"That would not be a good decision, Marcus. What will happen if you decide to do that?"

"I'll smash the sucker, that's what."

"And, if you choose that behavior, Marcus, what will you earn?"

"I'll earn his ass and yours too if you get in my way!"

"Marcus, it's OK to be angry about Jason's coming. Getting used to someone new can be difficult. But I'm counting on you and everyone else to help me. Jason's going to be nervous. He knows that all of us already know each other. We can be friends with each other now because we've had time to work together and learn the rules. Jason will walk in here tomorrow not sure whether anyone will be his friend."

"Well, I'm not gonna be his friend."

"You might change your mind, but even if you don't, I'm hoping that you will make good decisions about how you act. Even If you're angry, the rule is still the same—no hurting people."

"Tomika, thank you for raising your hand."

"Marcus, I don't know why you're being so doggish. Maybe Jason won't like you either."

Marcus starts to jump out of his chair. I move toward him with my hand raised, palm facing forward to signal stop. Marcus clenches both fists and throws himself back down on his seat.

"Tomika, it is true that Jason may decide not to like any of us. But the most important thing for us to do now is focus our attention on what we can do that will be helpful. Let's get back to our list of positive things we can do. Kevin said we could say hello. Tomika said we could ignore inappropriate behavior. Anything else? Tommy?"

"Help him learn where to go."

"OK, Tommy. I like that suggestion. Since you're our leader tomorrow, will you help Jason learn his way around?"

"Yeah."

"Thank you, Tommy. Anyone else? Lydel?"

"Tell him about earning money and our store."

"Right, Lydel. He needs to know about the good things we have here."

"Jonathan, you've been so quiet. Do you have any suggestions?"

"I just think we should be nice to him. I was so afraid my first day. I still get afraid in regular class sometimes 'cause I don't know the other kids yet. I just think we should be friends."

"Yeah. And what if he kicks you in the butt! You gonna be his friend then?"

"Marcus, that's enough! I like the way most of you are willing to give Jason a chance. He might be quiet the first few days or he might start acting up right away. Whichever way he acts, he'll be trying to find out about us. We have a responsibility to set a good example for him."

"But, why is he coming to our class?"

"Do you mean, why is he in a class for students with behavior problems?"

"Yeah. What did he do bad?"

"Jason needs extra help learning to follow directions and learning to handle his anger appropriately."

"He's not retarded, is he?"

"No, Kevin, he's not retarded. We've talked about all the different types of special education. None of you is retarded. Retardation is nothing to make fun of, though. Who remembers what it means to have a mental disability?"

"It means that it takes you longer to learn stuff."

"Right. What does gifted mean?"

"It means you learn stuff real fast."

"OK, what does learning disabled mean?"

"It means that you're really smart, but you have trouble with one or two things."

"And what about behavior disordered? Does that mean that you are crazy or have a mental disability?"

All of them in unison scream, "No-o-o-o-o-o!"

"That's right! What does it mean, Tomika?" "It means that we need extra help learning how to behave."

"OK. So, Jason is like that, too. Are we going to help him?" "Yeah!"

"Yeah!"

That yeah was unanimous. Even Marcus joined in the chorus. Minor scrimmages may be on the horizon, but the first battle is over. We're on our way.

Analyzing elements of the classroom environment with a Classroom Climate Checklist is an effective and unobtrusive method for improving students' behavior. The checklist provided on the following pages serves as a quick reference for the elements discussed in this chapter. Additional information on effective behavioral interventions and a Behavior Management Checklist are provided in Chapter 4.

Exhibit 2-1. Classroom Climate Checklist

Instructions: Place a check in the blank next to each item that represents a characteristic of your classroom setting, processes, and plans. Insert other information requested in the spaces provided.

Physical Setting

___   Are the walls, floors, and furniture clean and in good repair?

___   Is the furniture adjusted to the proper size for the students?

___   Are bulletin boards and other visual aids at an appropriate height?

___   Are rules, routines, and procedures posted in a manner that is easy to see?

___   Are rules, routines, and procedures posted in a manner that all can read or understand?

___   Are unnecessary and distracting items removed from view and reach?

___   Are materials organized and easily accessible?

___   Do students have secure and adequate spaces for personal storage?

___   Is the furniture arranged to meet instructional goals for grouping?

___   Are areas of the room activity specific?

___   Are the lighting and room temperature appropriate?

___   Is the room an appropriate size for the number of students and the activities planned?

___   Are there choices for student seating arrangements (small group, independent)?

___   Is there space for prominent display of student work?

___   Are items on the bulletin boards and wall academically focused and updated regularly?

___   Is the room attractive and inviting?

___   Has furniture been placed to decrease traffic flow challenges?

___   Have pencil sharpeners and trash cans been placed to decrease student distraction?

Scheduling

___   Is the schedule of activities posted and reviewed regularly?

___   Are independent tasks for students to complete when entering the room posted and accessible?

___   Are transition and non-instructional activities posted and reviewed regularly?

___   Are high and low preference activities alternated?

___   Are high and low interaction activities alternated?

___   Are critical activities scheduled at the most optimum time of the day?

___   Are choices for acceptable activities posted for students who complete an activity early?

___   Are the materials for acceptable activities accessible?

___   Is there a method for re-evaluating the schedule regularly?

___   Is there a method for posting changes to the schedule?

Instructional Planning

___ Are lesson objectives developed based on students' functioning levels?

___ Are assignments relevant and meaningful to students?

___ Are materials that students will be expected to use independently selected based on the students' academic achievement levels (reading and math)?

___ Are lesson plans designed to provide options based on student preferences and needs?

___ Are timelines adequate for the tasks planned?

___ Are classroom materials, equipment, and space allotments adequate for the tasks?

___ Do plans include methods for communicating the big ideas in lessons and units?

___ Are methods included for assisting students in relating new objectives to previously mastered material?

___ Are learning strategies that help students organize, remember, and use information included in the plans?

___ Are strategies for assisting students in learning new skills and concepts designed to allow for the gradual removal of support as students reach higher levels of mastery?

___ Are connections among the concepts taught in different subject areas directly identified for students?

___ Are review and reinforcement activities planned frequently to allow students to gain fluency with individual skills and retain content cumulatively over time?

Instructional Delivery

___ Are task directions clear and brief?

___ Are oral directions paired with pictures, icons, or written words that students can read?

___ Is the pace of instruction appropriate for the needs of all students?

___ Is sufficient time allotted for demonstration and explanation?

___ Is the time allotted for a specific activity adjusted to meet the needs of all students?

___ Do students have known choices for appropriate activities if they complete a task early?

___ Are nonpunitive provisions made for students who need more time?

___ Are the methods for introducing new content selected with regard for the needs of the students (e.g., manipulatives, audio-visual aids)?

___ Are student checks for understanding conducted frequently?

___ Are strategies used to direct students' attention to important details?

___ Are students grouped according to their instructional needs?

___ Is sufficient time provided for guided practice?

___ Is specific academic praise provided during guided practice?

___ Is corrective feedback provided promptly and positively during guided practice?

___ Is sufficient time provided for independent practice?

___ Is specific academic praise provided during independent practice?

___ Is corrective feedback provided promptly and positively during independent practice?

___ Is the most appropriate instructional strategy (e.g., direct instruction, cooperative learning) used given the content and mastery levels of the students?

Of the instructional tasks listed below, check those that result in the highest level of student engagement for the majority of students:

____ Highly structured independent work
____ Cooperative learning
____ Recall tasks (math facts, fill-in-the-blank)
____ Peer tutoring
____ Comprehension tasks (multiple choice)
____ Teacher-directed instruction
____ Application tasks (problem-solving)
____ Computer-assisted instruction
____ Evaluation tasks (rating self, others, or items on a predetermined criteria)

Additional Anecdotal Information Relative to Classroom Climate

_____

_____

_____

_____

_____

_____

_____

_____

3

Scheduling

Scheduling can be one of the most difficult aspects of the job to control. Many students have multiple disabilities requiring "pull-outs" during the day for speech therapy, physical therapy, or personal counseling. One or more students may be mainstreamed for all or part of the day. Physical education, music, art, and library time may also add to scheduling difficulties.

Many scheduling details are beyond the control of the teacher. Once a skeleton schedule of the typical week for each student and the group as a whole is established, the teacher can set up a workable instruction plan.

If students come into the classroom one at a time on their own in the morning, a quiet, highly structured activity that requires no teacher assistance is best. Copying spelling words; writing in a personal journal; copying a weekly poem, song, or recipe; doing math facts drills; matching patterns; illustrating a "thought of the day"; and solving an academically oriented puzzle are all possibilities.

If students enter the room together, a highly structured question-and-answer period before starting lessons can help them make the transition from the bus to the classroom.

Students need an introductory period every morning to review the rules in a positive manner, discuss the day's activities, and prepare for any unexpected changes.

As the daily schedule proceeds, strike a balance between individual and group activities. Whole group activities such as academic discussions, experiments, cooking, art, music, PE, and lunch can easily become over-stimulating for some students. However, isolation does not allow the students to learn more appropriate social behavior.

Expecting more self-control than the students are capable of reinforces negative self-concepts. Follow active periods with quiet, highly structured activities. Keep alternate plans for any activity in mind. Always having high-interest, self-structuring activities available can give the teacher and ultimately the students a sense of purpose, control, and security. One way I manage this task is to have a large, brightly colored file box within easy reach. Folders of instructional theme related materials are kept in that box for times when the lesson plan scheduled for a particular time period would be impossible to implement due to unforeseen behavioral outbursts or lack of group cooperation for one reason or another. Word puzzles, math sheets that include a secret message written in code that must be deciphered to be read, cut and paste activity sheets related to concept development in a content area, and spelling tasks that require the use of stencils, markers, glitter, or alphabet macaroni are examples of high interest, self-structuring alternatives to group lessons.

The following daily schedule illustrates the process of blending academic and behavioral needs. Notice that activities are never scheduled for more than 20-30 consecutive minutes and that active vs. passive and interactive vs. independent activities are alternated to decrease sensory deprivation or overload.

Exhibit 3.1 Sample Daily Schedule

Time

8:00-8:15   Suggested Independent Activities for Each Morning

Monday	Copy and illustrate a "Thought for the Week."
Tuesday	Academically oriented puzzle on a seasonal or holiday theme.
Wednesday	Copy and illustrate a seasonal poem or song of the week.
Thursday	Review spelling words with the aid of a previously taught memory game in preparation for the practice test.
Friday	Use the chart of the weekly recipe for the cooking activity as the reference point. Provide students with grocery store advertisments from the newspaper. Have them list ingredients for making the recipe and compute the total cost of purchasing the ingredients.

8:15-8:30   Attendance and opening announcements with a brief review
                             of class rules and the day's activities

8:30-8:40   Rapid-fire oral drill of calendar or math skills

8:40-8:45   One minute timed math quiz on individually determine math facts
                             followed by immediate feedback and charting of progress

8:45-9:00   Whole group math instruction in problem-solving

9:00-9:30   Independent skill practice using individualized materials

9:30-9:45   Bathroom breaks and recess or stretch break

9:45-10:00   Rapid-fire oral word drill. Make it fun by awarding points for
                             each correct answer. For talk-outs, erase one point. Each student
                             can have a different set of cards and still participate in the group

game to accommodate differing ability levels. To encourage a reluctant student to participate, award one point for attempting to read the word and another point if the response is correct. For oral drill of word attack skills, use cubes with consonants, consonant blends, and/or vowels on them. Students can earn points by thinking of words that start, end, or have the same vowel sound as the letters that come up when the cube is rolled.

10:00-10:30	Independent reading practice
10:30-10:40	Orally correct two to four incorrectly written sentences. Students recite rules to justify the changes as the teacher makes corrections on the board.
10:40-10:50	Whole group pre-writing activity

Examples:
1. Make word walls of words that relate to the assigned topic.
2. Read a brief story and discuss possible characters, setting, and plot.
3. Discuss events from a recent movie or field trip.
4. Brainstorm creative ideas.
5. Complete a pre-writing graphic organizer.

10:50-11:15	Independent writing
11:15-11:30	Partners edit and share writings
11:30-12:00	Lunch, bathroom break, and a brief evaluation of morning behavior and academic achievement
12:00-12:15	Read aloud
12:15-12:45	Science
12:45-1:15	Social Studies
1:15-1:30	Recess or stretch break and bathroom
1:30-1:45	Sing and/or listen to quiet music while reading silently a self-selected book.

1:45-2:15 Affective lesson

Use this time to teach new skills, review behavioral goals, individual and group progress, and group issues. One day per week can be devoted to a reward activity such as art, cooking, or outside games related to academic content. This activity can be earned by achieving a weekly behavior goal or by completing a predetermined amount of academic work.

Weekly Plans might look like this:

Exhibit 3.2. Sample Weekly Plan

Monday Review previously learned social skill and introduce a new skill if the students are ready to learn a new skill. Role play, puppets, and/or the examination of a related story or children's movie can be used to enhance the learning process.

Tuesday Review the targeted social skill and play a game or engage in a simulation that requires the application of the skill.

Wednesday Explore the thoughts and emotions that accompany events related to the targeted social skill through the use of journals, games, discussions, and/or simulations.

Thursday Examine each student's progress toward individual and group goal attainment relative to the targeted social skill(s) taught and the class expectations. Use this time to help students chart their progress in their journals.

Friday Reward activity and/or center activity. Students who earned the reward activity can participate in that while those who did not earn the activity engage in a center assignment designed to reinforce a desired behavior. Center activities might include designing a behavior monitoring chart with the help of a computer program, listening to a taped story about a child with a similar behavior who learned to manage that behavior more appropriately, and/or completing paper and pencil tasks designed to assist the student in learning from his or her mistakes.

A Note of Caution: Do everything possible to set the students up for success. They should have a sense of accomplishment when they earn the reward activity but should not be expected to be perfect in order to earn it. If a student consistently falls short of the criteria for earning the reward activity, he or she will experience an overwhelming sense of failure and will not attempt to perform successfully. It is appropriate to require different behaviors and levels of competence for individual students. If the student is capable of meeting the criteria and does not perform adequately, however, do NOT include the student in the activity. It is better to establish no criteria from the beginning and include everyone than to initially establish criteria and then fail to follow through. In addition, it is important to remember that some students will not like the planned activity. To avoid having those students act inappropriately as a strategy for being excluded from an activity they dislike, offer positive alternatives for them to earn or engage the group in a brainstorming session to find an activity all agree is worth pursuing.

A list of suggested Affective Education materials is provided in the Appendix that aligns with the instructional plan outlined above.

Students need to see an illustrated representation of the daily schedule to help them self-monitor and anticipate changes in activity level or daily routines. A sample of a partial daily schedule for student use is outlined below. Pocket charts are handy ways to display these daily schedules.

Today's Schedule

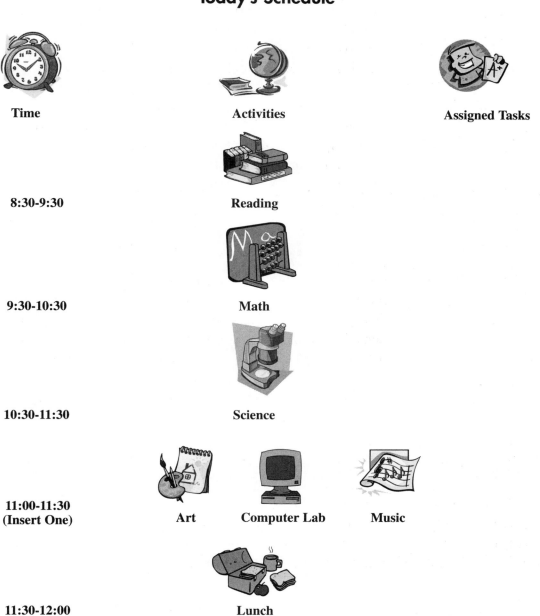

Time	Activities	Assigned Tasks
8:30-9:30	Reading	
9:30-10:30	Math	
10:30-11:30	Science	
11:00-11:30 (Insert One)	Art Computer Lab Music	
11:30-12:00	Lunch	

This allows for different words and pictures to be taken away or added as special classes (music, art, library, etc.) and other events change from day to day.

The consistent use of routines along with skillful balancing of activities can go a long way in establishing and maintaining classroom order. Jason's first day in class illustrates the effectiveness of following an established plan.

ANECDOTE

As I get to my room to organize myself before the buses roll in, I find Ms. Dodd waiting with Jason.

"Hello, Ms. Dodd. Jason, I'm so glad to meet you!"

Ms. Dodd gives me a warning glance as I move toward them.

"Jason, I'd like to show you your seat."

"Shut up you white ass, snot-sucking, honky bitch!"

"Ms. Dodd, have you and Jason had a chance to look around?"

"No. We've only been here a few minutes."

"Well, the class really worked hard to get things ready for you, Jason. This is your desk. We have a bulletin board space for you over here, and your point sheets and charts will be kept in this folder."

"Who gives a shit?"

"I'd also like to show you what your points will earn."

Each time I point to a store item, he mutters another string of profanity. His eyes are glued to every move I make, so for now I ignore his words.

After a brief introduction to our classroom standards and routines, I leave Ms. Dodd and Jason to wait for the class on the bus ramp.

Jason certainly curses proficiently. Most kids wait a day or two before showing me how they earned their behavior disorder status. This initial "honeymoon" period gives me time to let them receive some positive attention from me before I have to seem mean in their eyes. Jason is determined to make it impossible for me to put money in his bank either literally or figuratively. Without some positives, however, we're nothing more than sparring partners. And what about the class? Jason is definitely not on a campaign to win friends. I'm glad I wore boots today. I feel ankle-kicking, toe-stomping tantrums in the air.

The class files into the room more quietly than usual today. I invite Jason to join us at his desk. He refuses.

Jason, you may sit with Ms. Dodd for now if you like, but you will not earn points or money till you come to your seat." I might as well establish limits now. He isn't wasting any time showing me his anger; I won't waste any time letting him know where I stand.

"Don't even look at me, you wide-eyed whore! I don't give a shit about your points or your money."

The class looks at me to see what will happen.

"Thank you, class, for waiting patiently while I explain the rules to Jason. Here's a bonus nickel for each of you for being so appropriate. I'm sure when Jason is ready he'll join us."

The usual rapid-fire question-and-answer period begins. After a few minutes, Jason gets so caught up in the spirit of the game that he raises his hand to answer a question.

"Jason, I'd love to call on you, but you need to be in your seat first."

His hand slides down to his lap as he tries to decide what to do. With the whole class watching, he's under too much pressure to respond, so I continue our morning game with the others.

Jason quietly slips into his assigned seat just before we finish our calendar skills.

"Thank you for coming to your seat, Jason. Here's your dime for being in your assigned area and a penny if you can tell me what month we're in now."

"January."

"Absolutely right! There you are."

As I walk to the wall calendar, Jason tips his bank forward to see his money and smiles. Ms. Dodd gives me the thumbs-up sign from the back of the room as she leaves. I breathe a deep and very thankful sigh of relief.

4

Interventions

Because students with behavior problems tend to act in ways that get everyone's attention, it is easy to assume that the problem is the student's alone. Teachers, administrators, and parents respond to the problem by punishing the child and offering rewards for good behavior. While researchers have long known that people (and other living organisms) tend to behave in ways that most predictably get them what they want and help them avoid what they don't want, finding a solution to a student's long-standing behavior problem is not as simple as punishing "bad" behavior and rewarding "good" behavior. If individuals and groups were that easy to manage, no one would think a tough to reach, tough to teach student existed. Proponents of Positive Behavior Support (PBS) subscribe to the following research-based assumptions (Scott & Nelson, 1999; Sugai, Horner, Dunlap, Hieneman, Lewis, Nelson, Scott, Liaupsin, Sailor, Turnbull, Turnbull, Wickham, Wilcox, & Ruef, 2000):

1. Behavior is meaningful and is an attempt to communicate a want or need.

2. People behave in certain ways to get or avoid attention, sensory input (music, touch, movement, etc.), and/or tangible items (food, toys, etc.).

3. Behavior is contextual. The purpose and meaning of a behavior is related at least in part to the setting in which the behavior occurs.

4. In order to intervene successfully, the purpose or function of the behavior must be understood and addressed in the intervention plan.

5. Skill deficits indicate a need to teach new replacement skills.

6. Performance deficits indicate a need for increasing reinforcement when the behavior is exhibited.

7. Environmental contributors to the problem behavior should be assessed and addressed in the intervention plan.

8. In order to decrease an undesirable behavior or increase a desirable behavior the following components should be included in the Positive Behavior Support Plan process: (a) an analysis of current behaviors with regard to time, frequency, and place; (b) a hypothesis of the purpose or function of the behavior; (c) environmental supports, (d) educative interventions, (e) reinforcement, and (f) aversive consequences on a limited basis and as a last resort.

A great deal of support is currently available for educators, parents, and administrators who want to implement PBS at the individual student level. Online information can be obtained at www.pbis.org, and www.ldonline.org. Point cards, anecdotal records, and work sign-off sheets suggested in Chapter 2 would provide initial data that would be helpful in developing a hypothesis and would also be useful during on-going assessments of the intervention plan once it is implemented. Applying the PBS process at the classroom level prior to conducting lengthy functional behavioral assessments (FBA) on individuals can often reduce the number of students who need individualized plans.

Examine the Classroom Behavior Management Plan graphic organizer provided on the next page.

Exhibit 4.1. Building an Effective Classroom Management System

Rules	Routines/Procedures	Reinforcement System	Hierarchy of Aversive Consequences
Behaviors Handled in the Classroom	Behaviors Referred to the Office	Proactive Environmental Strategies	Educative Strategies

RULES, ROUTINES, AND PROCEDURES

Rules and expectations were discussed in detail in Chapter 2. Rules should be few in number, positively stated, and descriptive of observable, measurable behaviors. Routines and procedures include steps for lining up, sharpening a pencil, and gaining access to materials or privileges. The rules, expectations, routines, and procedures should be clearly posted and illustrated.

PROACTIVE ENVIRONMENTAL STRATEGIES

Proactive environmental strategies help students avoid unnecessary problems. Everything a teacher does in the course of a school day, from room arrangement and lesson planning to directly interacting with the students, is potentially an intervention. When problems arise, however, take time to analyze the situation. The easiest interventions to implement are ones, such as the following, that involve the environment.

1.   Move the desks farther apart.

2.   Use tape lines to designate activity-specific areas.

3. Use visual barriers where they are needed. File cabinets, rolling chalkboards, and book shelves are possibilities.

4. Increase or decrease the amount of lighting.

5. Put unnecessary items out of sight and, if possible, out of reach.

6. Organize materials for greater ease of use.

7. Adjust the schedule for a better balance of whole group and individual instruction.

8. Adjust the lessons to meet instructional and interest levels.

9. Adjust the materials to the needs and interests of the students. For instance, one child might hate to write but would willingly do the same work if he or she could cut and paste the appropriate responses on a worksheet from a list of possible responses. Similarly, crayons might be considered too infantile by another child. That child could use markers, colored pencils, or colored chalk. Appendix B includes sample worksheets that illustrate alternative ways to have a student practice the same skill.

10. Adjust the temperature of the room.

11. Adjust the height of visual aids.

12. Adjust tables, desks, and chairs to appropriate levels.

13. Divide assignments into two or more parts. Some students are able to handle two small worksheets with 10 problems on each page, but will have a tantrum if given one full worksheet with 20 problems on it. The work sign-off sheet in the Appendix is especially adaptable to this intervention. The teacher can use two initials to represent completion of a whole assignment. Before the student begins working, he or she can be told that there are two short assignments and that one initial will be awarded for each correctly completed part. This also works well for listening activities followed by written work. The students can receive one initial for actively listening and one for the written section.

Exhibit 4-2. Work Sign-off Sheet 1

Name _____   Week of _____

	Monday	Tuesday	Wednesday	Thursday	Friday
Opening Independent Work					
Group Meeting					
Reading					
Language Arts					
Lunch					
Specials (Music, Art, Library)					
Math					
Physical Education					
Science					
Social Studies					
Closing Activities					

Target Behavior(s)_____
_____
_____

Number of Sign-offs Needed to Earn the Friday Activity _____

Active listening should be clearly defined as sitting appropriately, making eye contact, and talking only at appropriate times. Review this definition with the students as often as necessary.

When environmental and instructional changes fail to eliminate a problem, individualized intervention plans can be used to meet specific children's needs. While teaching academic skills and concepts, the teacher must also keep eyes and ears alert for signs of stress in students. Sometimes simply moving closer to a student who is off task or upset can help bring the student's attention back to the immediate task. Giving a student a private signal to remember can also help. For example, when other students aren't around, tell a student that you will pull on your ear when you see him or her getting upset. That will be the cue to calm down or to pull his or her own ear to let you know that everything is OK. Nonverbal cues used in this way can set up a positive way to interact with specific students without interrupting instruction.

Another technique for helping with self-control is to give a student something to do in another area before a real problem begins. For example, when the student is getting irritated with another student who is calling him a name, ask the student who is being appropriate but getting irritated to take a note to the office.

Talking to students in a nonthreatening way, keeping them aware of their choices in any given situation, and focusing their attention on the appropriate decisions they are making even in the midst of a problem can help calm them down.

Avoid power struggles by making it clear that their behavior is under their control. A student who says "I'm not going to do this work, and you can't make me" needs to hear "Whether you work or not is your decision. If you decide to work, you will earn _____. If you decide not to work, you will earn _____. You decide what you want to earn."

Individual contracts can work within the context of the whole group plan. Keep any individual contract balanced with the total needs and abilities of the group. Students will be quick to point out unfair advantages or disadvantages.

For a student who frequently talks out or gets out of his or her seat without permission, a pocket on the student's desk top with strips of construction paper in it can help the student self-monitor. Determine how many times a specific behavior occurs in a given time period. If the average for the morning is 12, put 10 strips of paper in the student's desk pocket. Each time the behavior occurs, pull a strip out of the pocket or have the student do it. For each strip left in the pocket by the end of the specified time period, the student will earn a reward. Decrease the number of strips the student starts with each period as the student's behavior improves.

Another type of individual contract entails giving a student parts of a picture of a desired item to paste together as he or she masters increasingly difficult goals. When the picture is complete, the student earns whatever is pictured. Ladders, stepping stones, staircases, and tower designs with places for stickers that represent steps toward achievement can also be used. Samples of other individual contracts are provided in the Appendix.

Whole group interventions will meet the needs of most students most of the time. Incorporate classroom structure, scheduling, limit setting, and an established sense of purpose with an overall classroom behavior management plan.

Point cards, play money, tokens, work sign-off sheets, bonus points, a classroom store, checkbooks, savings accounts, cooking, art and music activities, and time-out are all tools of the trade. A sample point card and chart for record student progress are illustrated on the following pages.

Exhibit 4-3. Point Card

Name _____   **Date** _____

Keep hands, feet, and other objects to self.							Returned Signed Card
Complete tasks on time.							**Comments**
Target Behavior:							

Bonus Points | | | | | | |

Bus Points [ ]   **Lunch Points** [ ]

Teacher's Signature   **Student's Signature**   **Parent's Signature**

_____   _____   _____

(The back of the sheet can be used for recording anecdotal records.)

Exhibit 4-4. Target Behavior Data Collection Sheet

Student's Name _____   **Dates** _____

Target Behavior 1. _____

	M	T	W	TH	F	M	T	W	TH	F	M	T	W	TH	F	M	T	W	TH	F
100																				
90																				
80																				
70																				
60																				
50																				
40																				
30																				
20																				
10																				

Target Behavior 2. _____

	M	T	W	TH	F	M	T	W	TH	F	M	T	W	TH	F	M	T	W	TH	F
100																				
90																				
80																				
70																				
60																				
50																				
40																				
30																				
20																				
10																				

Target Behavior 3. _____

	M	T	W	TH	F	M	T	W	TH	F	M	T	W	TH	F	M	T	W	TH	F
100																				
90																				
80																				
70																				
60																				
50																				
40																				
30																				
20																				
10																				

General guidelines include:

1. Keep it simple, clear, and concrete.

2. Make all positives contingent on appropriate behavior.

3. Keep students' responsibility and power of choice at the core of each part of the plan.

In the classroom described in this book, play money is used. One point on a daily card equals one cent. Students keep banks on their desks made from empty milk cartons. Each month the students decorate new ones with seasonal designs. Bonus points are awarded with coins. Students count their money at the end of each day. Touching someone else's bank results in the contents of the offender's bank being emptied, with an opportunity to earn the money back with exceptional behavior. Also, playing with your own money would result in that money being taken.

The classroom store is open every Monday, Wednesday, and Friday afternoon during the first quarter of the school year. As students understand the system and become interested in purchasing more expensive items or activities the number of times the store is open per week decreases. Each student's balance is kept in a savings account on a section of the chalkboard. Checks are written from the account on store days. The addition and subtraction for the account are done by each student before the student receives selected store items. Students are permitted to save money if they do not have enough to buy a desired item. Lay-a-way plans are also permitted as long as the student has enough money to make a payment each store day.

The plan includes point card procedures, recordkeeping of daily points, target behaviors, work sign-off sheets, bonus point procedures, ways to earn special activities, a menu of reinforcers, and a menu of consequences. This is a sample—a springboard for creative ideas.

Page 46 shows a sample point sheet. The teacher may decide to divide the day into time periods or subject and activity periods. The boxes for recording points earned are in six columns for each of three behaviors. Two rows of six boxes in each section represent 30 minute increments of time. The teacher can add pictures to represent activities for each of the columns or write times over those columns. Each column represents an hour in the school day. Younger students seem to understand subject and activity period names better than times. A possible 12 points can be earned each half hour. If a student exhibits the desired behaviors during a half-hour time period, place 2 points in each box corresponding to the 3 behaviors. If the student requires more than a verbal reminder, the student would earn 1 point for that particular behavior. If the student continued to be noncompliant, a 0 would be recorded for that behavior. There are a total of 72 points for classroom behavior each day. In addition, the student could earn 4 bus points for the A.M. bus ride, 4 bus points for the P.M. bus ride, 10 points for returning a signed point card, and 10 points for appropriate lunch or cafeteria behavior. Target behavior(s) must be written in by the teacher each day. Even though a student may have more than three problem behaviors, only work on one or two at a time. Select the most dangerous or disruptive behaviors first. Possible target behaviors might include keeping hands and feet to oneself, using an appropriate volume of voice, using words to express feelings, using an appropriate tone of voice, putting items away neatly, keeping one's personal area organized, starting assignments on time, and using appropriate words to communicate ideas and feelings.

A Target Behavior Data Collection Sheet chart is shown on page 47. This chart has room for 4 weeks' worth of point sheet totals. At the end of each day, the teacher will draw a line on the chart for the correct total and day. The student will color a bar graph to illustrate his or her behavior progress. Students often like to use seasonal colors, since these charts are on a special bulletin board in the room. Students who are trying to earn mainstreaming privileges benefit from having a line drawn horizontally across the percentage area they must achieve in order to be mainstreamed. At the end of each month, a photocopy of the chart is made for the teacher's records. Students are then permitted to take the colorful copy home. Some parents like to use these charts along with the daily point sheets to help motivate the students with rewards at home. Parents must be reminded to accentuate the positive. Periodically remind them that the point sheets and monthly charts are tools of communication. Help them see that even though a student may have low points for a particular day, he or she still may have made good choices.

The following lists of reinforcers and aversive consequences or punishments are only a start. Ask the students what they want to earn. Be observant to detect their least favorite activities. For the plan to work, there must be things students want to avoid as well as things they want to earn.

REINFORCERS

Primary reinforcers include food items and drinks. These work best with younger students and with any age when stress factors are high. Permission from parents is sometimes needed. Primary reinforcers might include the following:

Candy	Juice	Fruit
Crackers	Soda	Cookies
Cake	Pizza	Chips
Pretzels	Ice cream	Marshmallows

Secondary reinforcers include tangible items. It is wise to discuss student preferences with the class to avoid purchasing too many unwanted items. Free samples and donations are often available. Some suggested secondary reinforcers are:

Posters	Erasers	Cars
Dolls	Stickers	Games
Notebooks	Pens	Markers
Sports cards	Jewelry	Clothing
Visors	Sunglasses	Cologne
Bubble bath	Caps	Silly straws
Nail polish	Pencil	

Social reinforcers are the highest level of reinforcement. It is not recommended that groups begin earning these at first unless adult supervision is always available. The students will be earning time and the right to use whatever materials are necessary. Points can be paid by the minute. For instance, 1 minute of video game time could equal 5 points. The student would need 50 points in order to buy 10 minutes of playing time. Completing school work may also need to be a prerequisite to playing. Some suggested social reinforcers include:

Painting	Game Time	Listening to Tapes or Records
Clay	Computer	Visiting another classroom
Models	Library	Helping in the office
Coloring	Films	Playing outside

HIERARCHY OF AVERSIVE CONSEQUENCES

Students with behavior problems respond best when a predictable, consistently enforced system is followed. In addition to clearly posted and illustrated expectations, rules, routines, procedures, and opportunities for reinforcement, a hierarchy of responses to noncompliance should be provided. Some teachers use a card system. Each student has a pocket with three to five different colored cards representing steps in the hierarchy. Green often indicates that all is well. If a student requires more than one verbal warning, a yellow card is displayed. Cool-off might be indicated with a blue card, In Class Suspension with an orange card, and office referrals or calls to parents with a red card.

A plan that has worked well for me is described below.

1. Use a system of *s and /s next to each student's name on the chalkboard to award bonus points and issue warnings. The teacher can decide how many bonus points each * is worth, whether or not the /s will represent fees for disruption of the educational process, and how frequently to award *s. Other advantages of this system include (a) nonverbal, visual cues that do not require a break in the instructional process and (b) a clearly defined way for students to monitor their own behavior. Bus behavior and homework rewards can also be built into this system.

Example	Key
Joe **/****	Homework = **
Sue **** // *	Bus behavior = ***
Mark * * / * * * *	

Bonus point totals for each student would be +16 for Joe, + 11 for Sue, and + 16 for Mark. Draw a vertical line through all rows at the end of each period to keep track of points earned. Three /s in one period would equal a 0 on the point sheet. Each afternoon, total the points for the day and then erase all but the names in order to be ready for the next day.

2. Use the *s and /s to as indicators of when students will earn 0s on the point card and/or removal from an activity to sit in Cool-off. In Cool-off students may continue to work if they are calm. They continue to earn points if they are following directions. If they are not able to redirect their behavior within 5-15 minutes, they will be asked to sit in In Class Suspension/(ICS). Students can earn sign-offs on the work sign-off sheet, but no points. Removal to another classroom to complete independent work would be next on the hierarchy with calls to parents and administrative referrals being the last option. Each hierarchy should include a severe clause for behaviors that will result in immediate serious consequences. Generally, hurting others and leaving class without permission are the only two non-negotiable behaviors in the severe clause. If ICS or time out of the classroom is going to be used as an aversive consequence, remember to (a) limit the amount of time a student is excluded, (b) make the ICS and time out of the classroom as unstimulating as possible, and (c) make sure that the classroom activities and assignments are engaging.

Unless students seem to need individual point cards, avoid using them in large classes. A visual cuing system combined with consistent attention to positive behavior and predictable reactions to noncompliant behavior is often enough for most if not all of the students. Positive recognition of school appropriate behavior should occur at a rate of at least three positives for every redirective response. Redirective responses are not always considered reprimands by adults. They include statements such as "Please sit down." and "Please get out your book." Unless the environment is rich in positive interactions (smiles, pats on the back, verbal praise, etc.), students will perceive the teacher to be negative, nagging, and unlikable.

BEHAVIORS HANDLED IN THE CLASSROOM

Behaviors that can and should be handled in the classroom include talk-outs, profanity, off-task behaviors, and arguments between students. Establishing a classroom climate that includes everyone requires attention to disruptive behaviors in the context of that classroom culture. If students are not connected to peers and adults within the classroom, sending them to other adults for discipline usually has little effect.

BEHAVIORS REFERRED TO THE OFFICE

Behaviors that require immediate administrative attention are those that pose a danger to the student or others. Serious physical, attempts to hurt self and leaving class without permission represent safety issues. Administrators and teachers should determine prior to the beginning of the school year which behaviors warrant an administrative referral.

EDUCATIVE STRATEGIES

Educative strategies include all interventions that teach students new skills and concepts. Whole-group techniques that work well and provide flexibility for the teacher are as follows:

1. Teach students decision-making steps early. Within the first month of school, the class needs to know that the teacher has a plan for dealing with whole-group problems.

    When several students become involved in a fight or loud argument, an effective way to calm the class is to follow these steps:

    a. Reward each student who is sitting quietly with bonus points or a small, edible reward. Let everyone know that sitting quietly will earn a reward.

    b. After 3 to 5 minutes, remove from the room students who will not sit quietly. If this is not possible, continue to reward the others until everyone is calm enough to continue. Another alternative is to have an aide take the students who are behaving appropriately out of the room for a little while. This will give the acting-out students an opportunity to settle down without losing face with their audience.

    c. Once everyone is sitting and ready to begin, list the decision-making steps on the chalkboard. Explain to the class that you are interested in hearing each person's point of view about the upsetting incident. Remind them that each person will have a chance to speak; bonus points will only be given for appropriate behavior; and each person is to limit what he or she says to what was felt, seen, and heard personally. No accusations or name calling will be allowed.

    d. Give the students time to respond to the following decision-making steps as related to the specific incident:

        1. Identify the problem, goal, and/or feeling.

        2. List alternative actions.

        3. Pick the most appropriate alternative(s).

        4. Act on your decision.

        5. Evaluate.

By the time each student has responded, the group will be calm and ready to make a decision about how to handle any future problems. This technique requires careful monitoring by the teacher, especially in the beginning.

While it will not immediately put a stop to problems in a group, the individual students and the class as a whole grow tremendously through consistent use of this process. Knowing that each person's perceptions of the event, feelings, and ideas about how to resolve the issue will be recognized as well as being given the opportunity to problem-solve together with the teacher strengthens the students' feelings of self-control, self-respect, and willingness to cooperate.

It is possible for any type of class to learn this process. Students eventually begin the process and carry it out completely with little or no help from the teacher. It will only work, however, if the teacher consistently recognizes and rewards appropriate behavior.

The steps can also be written out on a worksheet. Students can be given the worksheet to fill out instead of participating in a discussion if that is thought to be more productive in some cases.

2. Establish group goals that encourage individuals to correct their own behavior. Make it clear that group rewards will be forfeited if inappropriate behavior is used to put pressure on classmates to conform. For example, one group goal could be that everyone will handle his or her problems quickly so that time-out is not needed. Each day that all members of the group are able to stay in class all day, even if minor problems occur, the whole class will receive a reward. Other group goals might include appropriate bus behavior, turning in homework, or using words instead of fists when angry. If group goals are carefully monitored to guard against negative peer pressure, this technique can build a spirit of cooperation and achievement.

   The teacher must establish realistic goals for this to work. An extremely aggressive class will only feel more defeated and angry if a goal to stop all fighting is set when fights are frequent and individuals within the group have not learned alternative self-control methods. Build the group up slowly with short-term goals first. For example, if there are no talk-outs during morning announcements, the group will earn _____. To avoid a blow-up by the other group members if one student fails to follow through, award bonus points or a small, edible reward to those who were following directions. Remind them that their appropriate behavior helps classmates who have not yet mastered the self-control required.

3. Produce and display group projects on a regular basis. As the students learn to cooperate with each other, they will need a way to get positive recognition from others. For example, have the students make model Indian and Pilgrim villages with pretzels glued to milk cartons, sticks, paper, cloth, and dug-out canoes made

from bars of soap, giving everyone an opportunity to contribute. The group can make maps, reports, and even a class book about the project. Invite other classes to view it or put it on display in the office or school library. Making a tape-recorded rap song, radio play, or selection of songs to be played over the school intercom is another way to get positive school-wide recognition. While these whole-group projects take extra planning, they are well worth the effort.

4. Select literature to read aloud or movies to view and discuss that illustrates a common group problem. Discuss the characters, setting, conflict, and resolution of the story as it unfolds each day. Students gain many insights while building vocabulary and an increased interest in literature. One upper elementary group obsessed with racial prejudice and fighting responded extremely well to a discussion of *The Call of the Wild*. After finishing one chapter, a student exclaimed, "Those dogs act just like us!" The class launched into a discussion that lasted as long as the book took to read. Fights decreased, respect for individuals increased; and, surprisingly, empathy began to develop among the students.

When selecting literature or movies, the following guidelines have been found to increase effectiveness:

- Select literature that illustrates one or more of the universal values identified as (a) compassion, (b) honesty, (c) fairness, (d) responsibility, and (e) respect (Kidder & Born, 1999).

- Select literature that illustrates one or more of the six components of interpersonal cognitive problem-solving skills identified as (a) consequential thinking, (b) means-ends thinking, (c) alternative thinking, (d) cause and effect thinking, and (e) perspective taking (Shure, 1992).

- Select literature that facilitates respect for cultural and ethnic diversity (Stoodt-Hill & Amspaugh-Corson, 2001).

- Select literature that portrays people with disabilities as (a) capable of growth and change, (b) worthy of respect, and (c) coping realistically with the challenges portrayed (Kupper, 1994; Prater, 1999).

- Select films that (a) offer hope, (b) reframe problems, (c) provide positive role models, (d) assist in identifying & reinforcing internal strengths, (e) improve communication, and (f) prioritize values (Hesley & Hesley, 1998).

Exhibit 4-5. Selected Stories, Films, and Other Instructional Resources

Primary (Grades 1 - 3)

- *On Monday When It Rains* by Cherryl Kachenmeister (Identifying feelings)
- *Knots on a Counting Rope* by Bill Martin, Jr. & John Archambault (Coping with loss)
- *Let's Be Enemies* by Janice May Udry (Conflict with a friend)
- *The Island of Skog* by Steven Kellogg (Fear of the unknown & conflict resolution)
- *The Hating Book* by Charlotte Zolotow (Conflict with a friend)
- *The Fight* by Betty Boegehold (Conflict & consequences)
- *An American Tale*
- *The Butter Battle*
- *The Wizard of Oz*

Intermediate (Grades 4 - 5)

- "The King and His Hawk" in *The Children's Book of Virtues* by W. J. Bennett (Anger)
- *Hope* by Isabell Monk (Pride in cultural heritage & overcoming prejudice)
- *Crazy Lady* by Jane Leslie Conly (Conflict resolution & overcoming disabilities)
- *Chicken Sunday* by Patricia Polacco (Love, friendship, & overcoming prejudice)
- *The True Story of the Three Little Pigs* by Jon Scieszka (Alternative perspectives in a conflict)
- *On My Honor* by Marion Dane Bauer (Dealing with loss & conscience)
- *What Jamie Saw* by Carolyn Coman (Dealing with domestic abuse)
- *October Sky*
- *Where the Red Fern Grows*
- *Charlie and the Chocolate Factory*

Secondary

- *The Hatchet* by G. Paulsen (Coping with loss and problem-solving)
- *That Was Then This Is Now* by S. E. Hinton (Conflict: Loyalty to a friend or to personal goals)
- *Call of the Wild* by Jack London (Conflict and coping with loss)
- *A Girl Named Disaster* by Nancy Farmer (Coping, loss, and survival)
- *People Profiles* (Series: Biographies of famous people)
- *Rudy*
- *Dangerous Minds*
- *Apollo 13*

DEALING WITH SETBACKS

In a classroom for students with behavior disorders, it is important to learn to pat yourself on the back for small steps forward. Learning to accept setbacks is also essential. In the following anecdote, Jason once more illustrates the need for teacher flexibility in selecting interventions.

ANECDOTE

Jason manages himself well for most of the morning. His interactions are stiff and controlled, but appropriate. After lunch, midway through our science lesson, Jason's need to take control overtakes him. He throws a tack and refuses to pick it up.

"Jason, throwing things is not appropriate in the classroom. Please pick up the tack by the count of four. If you decide not to, I will help you. You have to the count of four to make up your mind. One.. . two.., three. . ., four...."

Jason walks halfway to the tack. Then he stops and refuses to follow through.

"Jason, let's pick it up together. I will hold your hand and walk with you." Jason's hand is limp. At first he walks slowly with me. Without warning, he begins to kick, scratch, bite, and punch.

"Jason, I cannot allow you to hurt me, yourself, or anyone else. If you cannot stop yourself, I will hold you till you can. You have to the count of three. One. . ., two. . ., three."

On three, I half carry, half drag him to the rug. Jonathan is mainstreamed at the time. Kevin is out for personal counseling. Tomika sits quietly at her desk working puzzles. Lydel begins running into walls, yelling, "My protection! Help! Help!" Tommy stares out the window while Marcus encourages Jason to "beat my ass."

Because Ms. Agnew has left early today, I send Tomika to get another teacher to take the others to another room for a while. In the meantime, I wrestle to get Jason into a safe restraint position. Jason is strong and wiry. Before I manage to get him into a secure position, he kicks me, scratches my arm and his own face, pulls out some of his own hair, and urinates on both of us. I continue to talk as calmly as I can to Jason and Lydel.

"Lydel, it's OK. Ms. Thomas is coming. We won't let anyone hurt you."

"Jason, I know you're upset. Take deep breaths. I won't hurt you. I just want you to calm down."

Ms. Thomas finally comes for Lydel, Tomika, Marcus, and Tommy. They will stay with her for a while.

"Jason, can you tell me what you're thinking?" He stops struggling as soon as the others leave. I am hoping to find out what this tantrum is all about.

"No one likes me."

"You think you don't have any friends?"

"No! Everyone hates me. You hate me. You scream at me all the time."

"Jason, I can't remember ever screaming at you. When did I scream at you?"

"I don't know. Maybe you didn't. But you will. Everyone does. And you hate me anyway."

"I've only known you for one day. So far, I've seen a strong, healthy, nice-looking young man who likes to do well on his schoolwork and who knows more about math than most of his classmates. I don't hate anything about you."

"But I kicked you and called you names."

"Yes, you did."

"My other teachers said, 'He's just too bad. Get him out of here.'"

"I'm not your other teachers. I don't want you or anyone else to get hurt in here. When you're angry, you have extra energy. I think I need to teach you better ways to use that energy. That's why you're in this room with me. I knew you needed help with that. I told Ms. Dodd I wanted you to come to my class."

"No you didn't!"

"Yes I did! You can ask her. I don't hate you, Jason. I don't hate any child for needing extra help learning things. But I won't let you hurt anyone, either. Now, what can you do with that extra energy?"

"Run!"

"OK."

"Beat pillows!"

"OK."

"But we don't have any in here."

"No, we don't. Can you think of any other ideas?"

"I could hit the wall instead of people."

"That might hurt you. I like your idea about running. You may ask Ms. Agnew to take you out for a run when she is here and you feel the need. Other things you might try would be sitting in a chair and wiggling your feet or scribbling on a paper when you feel the extra energy building up. Now please pick up the tack."

"Here it is." Jason's tear-stained face has a real smile on it.

In the weeks that follow, Jason and I have two more similar episodes. After that, he knows me well enough to let the other interventions work for him. In the year and a half I work with him, he never becomes physically aggressive again. He also never needs hospitalization.

TOUCHING

A note about touching students who are upset is needed here. The age and maturity level of the child must be considered. When Jason refused to pick up the tack he had thrown, an alternative to walking him to the tack by holding his hand would have been charging him points for having someone else pick up the tack. Jason then would not have required contact. He still might have attacked me or a classmate anyway. Verbal and physical aggression were his primary ways of dealing with anger. Holding his hand in a gentle way before his blow-up gave him an opportunity to find out through touch that I had no intention of hurting him. Jason was 8. This would not work as well with a middle school or even upper elementary student. Base choices given to students on their age, physical size, emotional maturity, and ability to understand.

It is also wise to remember that students will be unpredictable in their reactions. Kevin had been with me for one and a half years before he took any physical aggression out on me. Screaming, cursing, fighting with peers, tearing up school materials, and knocking over furniture were problems that Kevin had exhibited. He was making tremendous progress academically and behaviorally. I had become comfortable and a little too nonchalant with him. One day after recess, a hot, sweaty, and very angry Kevin returned to the room. He told me he was upset, and we talked a while. I misjudged how angry he really was. At one point I tapped him on the head with some papers and said, "Oh, come on, Kevin. It's OK."

It wasn't OK with Kevin. He flew out of his seat and punched me with all of his 8-year-old might right in the jaw. I was shocked. Impulsively, I grabbed his wrists and said in a quiet but firm voice, "Kevin, what are you doing?"

It took 6 weeks of wearing a splint to repair the damage to my jaw. But I learned a life-long lesson from my mistake.

Some students need more support than the classroom behavior management plan provides. A set of interventions called Kid Tools is available at www.kidtools.missouri.edu. This free, downloadable program includes externally controlled, shared control, and internally controlled interventions for students at the primary and intermediate levels. Kid Tools contains a menu of options that includes self-monitoring formats, individual behavioral contracts, and cognitive-behavioral interventions.

Chapter 5 addresses the importance of establishing and maintaining an instructional focus. In spite of behavior problems, a great deal of learning can and does occur with proper planning and support. Before examining instructional strategy options, use the Classroom Behavior Management Plan Checklist to fine tune any remaining gaps in the class-wide Positive Behavior Support system.

Exhibit 4-6. Classroom Behavior Management Plan Checklist

<u>Delineation of Roles</u>

List the behaviors that are handled in the classroom:

List the behaviors that are referred to an administrator:

How are behaviors that are referred to administrators documented?

<u>Rules: Behaviors that are expected at all times.</u>

___ Are the rules clearly different from procedures that are used for accessing an item or activity?
___ Are rules positively stated?
___ Is the number of rules limited to no more than 5?
___ Are the rules worded in observable and measurable terms?
___ Are the rules posted on a chart that is large enough for all to see?
___ Are the rules written in words that all can read and/or illustrated with graphics or icons?
___ Are rules taught and reviewed regularly?

<u>Routines: Procedures for entering, exiting, and accessing an item, assistance, or activity.</u>

___ Are methods and times for sharpening pencils, collecting lunch money, and accessing a pass
    to the restroom clearly posted?
___ Are sufficient opportunities provided for these routines?
___ Are provisions for special needs made with regard to the routines?
___ Are plans for exceptions to the routines and procedures provided for students (e.g., What
    happens if someone breaks his/her pencil lead before the end of class?)?
___ Are the methods and times for routines aligned with the rules of the class?
___ Are the methods and times for routines aligned with the instructional needs of the class?
___ Are routines taught and reviewed regularly?

Provisions for Monitoring, Teaching, and Acknowledging Behavior

Which behaviors are monitored?

How is the data recorded?

What methods are used to teach desired behaviors and rules?

What methods are used to reinforce students who model the desired behaviors?

___ Social reinforcer (praise)
___ Activities
___ Tangibles
___ Tokens/Points

How are items and activities selected?

___ Do students and parents have input in the selection of reinforcers?
___ What criteria is used for earning the reinforcers?
___ What criteria is used for using (spending) or obtaining the activities, tangibles, and/or tokens?
___ Is specific behavioral praise provided at a rate of four positives to every one corrective statement?
___ Is specific behavioral praise provided contingent on the demonstration of the desired behavior?
___ Are reinforcers (verbal, nonverbal, items, activities) available to all who earn them?
___ Are reinforcers varied and individualized?
___ Is the schedule of reinforcement varied to maximize effectiveness (constant while students are learning and intermittent after mastering a behavior)?
___ Is data on student performance displayed prominently?
___ Are reinforcement opportunities posted?

<u>Consequences for Behaviors That Violate Classroom Rules</u>

What specific behaviors would violate the classroom rules?

What consequences are used when a student violates a classroom rule?

___ Are the consequences for rule violation sequential?
___ Are the consequences for rule violation educative?
___ Are the consequences for rule violation preplanned and posted?
___ Are the consequences for rule violation explained and reviewed regularly?
___ Are consequences delivered in a calm, matter-of-fact manner?
___ Are students reminded of their choices in a calm, positive manner prior to an escalation in behavior?
___ Are consequences delivered consistently and in a timely manner?

What behavior management techniques and consequences are used in the classroom?

___ Planned Ignoring (for what?)
___ Nonverbal Warnings (gestures, icons, visual or auditory cues)
___ Verbal Warnings
___ Proximity control (adult moves closer to the student without interacting directly)
___ Antiseptic Bouncing (removing a student from a situation prior to problem escalation)
___ Humor
___ Direct Appeal (just ask the student to stop)
___ Restructure an activity/move a student's seat
___ Time-out
___ Referral
___ Loss of points and/or loss of access to materials, people, or activities
___ Parent Contact
___ Office Referral
___ Other (Explain)

What educative strategies are used in the classroom to teach students with skill deficits?

___ Behavior Bingo and other games designed to teach classroom rules
___ Think Sheet (problem-solving format for self-reflection)

___ Social Autopsy (discussion of the events leading to and including the problem with an emphasis on (a) increasing the student's awareness of social expectations and (b) helping the student generate solutions for future situations)

___ Social Stories (stories written to specifically address a social situation and solutions for an individual)

___ Social Skills Lessons (with a curriculum that includes modeling, feedback, role play, and homework)

___ Conflict Resolution Training

___ Aggression Replacement Training

___ Problem-solving Skills

___ Other (Explain)

5

Instructional Focus

Once a behavior management system is established and a skeleton schedule has begun to take shape, instructional planning can begin in earnest. The following statistics represent behavior management and instructional challenges for teachers that must be recognized and effectively managed in order for learning to occur:

1. Researchers estimate that 6% to 10% of the youth in the United States who are school age have serious emotional and behavioral problems (Brandenburg, Friedman, & Silver, 1990; Kauffman, 2001).

2. Approximately 6% of the school-aged population has been identified as having a learning disability.

3. Attention deficit hyperactivity disorder (ADHD) has been found to overlap with learning disabilities at a rate of 10% to 25% (Forness & Kavale, 2002).

4. Emotional and behavioral disorders has been found to overlap with ADHD at a rate of 25% to 50% (Forness & Kavale, 2002).

5. The United States Department of Health and Human Services (2001) reports that only 1% of the students with emotional and behavioral problems are served in special education programs.

6. Nearly 1 in 6 Americans do not speak English as their first language (Cohen & Cohen, 2001).

7. More than 2 million grandparents are raising their grandchildren (Cohen & Cohen, 2001).

8. One in 6 children live in poverty (Cohen & Cohen, 2001), which puts them at greater risk for developing health, learning, and behavior problems (Fujiura & Yamaki, 2000).

These factors increase the diversity of students' achievement levels and instructional needs. One way teachers have dealt with differing academic levels in the past has been to create a folder of work each day for each student. This method may be necessary for brief periods of time as limits are being set for a group, but having students sit alone at their desks as the teacher walks around helping them one at a time is a poor use of instructional time. Furthermore, it teaches students nothing about how to manage in a more typical classroom setting. With 10 students in a class, this arrangement only allows each student 6 instructional minutes per hour. In inclusion settings with 25-35 students in each class, the amount of instructional time per student each hour can drop to less than 2 minutes per student.

How can a teacher do anything else with so many academic levels in one small group? Fortunately, scholars at the National Center to Improve the Tools of Educators (NCITE) synthesized 30 years of research on instruction across all academic content areas (Kameenui, Simmons, Baker, Chard, Dickson, Gunn, Lin, Smith, & Sprick, 1994; Dixon, 1994; Dixon, Carnine, & Kameenui, 1992; Miller, Crawford, Harness, & Hollenbeck, 1994; Grossen, & Lee, 1994). They set aside debates on the merits of one philosophical approach over another and concerned themselves with a single critical question. Which empirically validated characteristics are essential to the efficacy of curriculum and instruction for diverse populations of students? The answer to this question was summarized in the identification of the Universal Access Principles for Instruction. These principles include (a) identifying major concepts, (b) activating prior knowledge, (c) utilizing conspicuous strategies, (d) providing mediated scaffolding, (e) strategically integrating content, and (f) engaging students in judicious review (Kameenui & Carnine, 1998).

The following procedures facilitate the inclusion of all six principles in the planning and implementation of instruction:

BIG IDEAS (EXPLICITLY IDENTIFIED MAJOR CONCEPTS)

Unit planning routines assist in maintaining instructional focus. Students benefit from having key concepts explicitly identified and placed in a framework that illustrates how the key concepts relate to the goals of the total unit (Boudah, Lenz, Bulgren, Schumaker, & Deshler, 2000; Joint Committee on Teacher Planning for Students with Disabilities, 1995; Wasta, Scott, Marchand-Martella, & Harris, 1999).

- Students have been given an overview of the key concepts and skills that they will be expected to know at the end of the unit currently being taught.

- Graphic organizers, icons, photographs, and/or key vocabulary illustrate the major concepts to be mastered and are displayed prominently in the classroom.

- Each lesson is aligned with one or more of the major concepts targeted for mastery.

- Students can identify how the current lesson aligns with the unit plan.

PREVIOUSLY MASTERED SKILLS & CONCEPTS (PRIMED BACKGROUND KNOWLEDGE)

Methods that assist students in the process of assimilating new information with prior knowledge are included in the planning and implementation of lessons (Joint Committee on Teacher Planning for Students with Disabilities, 1995; Hyerle, 1996; Tomlinson, 1999; Burke et al., 1998).

- Before beginning a lesson on a new topic or skill, students are engaged in instructional activities that assist them in identifying previously mastered concepts that are relevant to the new lesson objective.

- Timelines, charts, and other visual aids are used to illustrate connections among previously mastered concepts and skills and current lessons.

- Students have access to support materials such as dictionaries, reference books, multiplication charts, measurement conversion charts, and other items that would assist them in the transfer of prior knowledge to new or higher level concepts.

STRATEGIES FOR LEARNING (CONSPICUOUS STRATEGIES)

Experts in a particular field and students who have mastered a specific skill use processes at an automatic level that students with learning problems are often unable to identify for themselves. Making strategies and processes explicit increases student ownership and responsibility for progress (Joint Committee on Teacher Planning for Students with Disabilities, 1995; Hyerle, 1996; Tomlinson, 1999; Burke et al., 1998; Harris & Pressley, 1991).

- Unit plans and lesson plans identify complex concepts and skills.

- Strategies found to be helpful in the completion of complex tasks such as the use of graphic organizers and mnemonic devices are included in unit and lesson plan development.

- Evidence of student involvement with the development and implementation of conspicuous strategies is evident in classwork assignments, homework assignments, cooperative group products, and bulletin board displays.

INSTRUCTIONAL SUPPORTS (MEDIATED SCAFFOLDING)

Students often need assistance in developing organizational skills, in accessing information, in understanding complex concepts, and in demonstrating what they have learned. Strategies that support present levels of functioning and allow for the gradual withdrawal of support as higher levels of mastery are demonstrated facilitate motivation and increase students' rates of mastery (Joint Committee on Teacher Planning for Students with Disabilities, 1995; Hyerle, 1996; Tomlinson, 1999; Wasta et al., 1999).

- Unit plans and lesson plans identify complex concepts and skills.

- Routines for teaching strategies for complex task completion such as the use of graphic organizers and mnemonic devices are included in the unit and lesson plan development.

- Additional levels of support for targeted students are integrated into the overall plan for instruction and are available to all who may need them.

Example: Students with specific learning disabilities are often able to comprehend content presented orally, but have difficulty with reading fluency. They may benefit from listening to text on an audio tape if more than a few paragraphs or pages of reading are required in order to complete an assignment. Listening centers provide students with graduated levels of support. Students with reading fluency deficits, students with attention deficits, and students who learn best by listening even when their reading levels are adequate can access the level of support necessary for the task.

- Additional levels of support for targeted students are integrated into the overall plan for instruction. These strategies are designed to assist the student in (a) moving to a higher level of mastery, and/or (b) generalize skills across tasks, content areas, or settings.

Example: Specific students may have difficulty with organization. Highly structured methods for formatting their classwork, maintaining their calendar or day planner, and developing their content area notebooks may need to be established. A teacher, assistant, or peer buddy may need to provide (a) direct instruction in the specific organizational tasks targeted, (b) monitoring, and (c) acknowledgement of the use of the skill(s) for every defined task. The student should be given a checklist with icons or key words and phrases to help him/her self-check prior to receiving feedback from a peer or adult. As the student's proficiency increases, the number of steps listed on the checklist and the frequency of buddy or adult checks can be reduced. The completion of projects, cooperative learning tasks, and other complex, multi-step assignments might be facilitated by the same process with a whole class by providing multiple prompts during the first few assignments and gradually reducing the number of checkpoints and prompts used to cue and orient students as they demonstrate mastery.

CONTENT ORGANIZATION
(STRATEGIC INTEGRATION: SEQUENCED, PARALLEL, AND OVERLAPPING)

Strategic integration requires careful planning before beginning a unit of study. Students with learning difficulties do not make connections within and among content areas without assistance. Retention, skill mastery, and motivation are enhanced through content integration (Joint Committee on Teacher

Planning for Students with Disabilities, 1995; Hyerle, 1996; Tomlinson, 1999; Burke et al., 1998; Boudah et al., 2000).

- The scope and sequence of skills and concepts outlined in the text have been aligned with the known strengths and needs of the students in the class.

- Students' strengths and needs are assessed with regard to the unit scope and sequence.

- Unit and lesson plan development reflects a consideration of related skills and concepts being taught in other content areas.

- Concepts and skills are sequenced with a clear progression from concrete and simple to abstract and complex.

- Parallel themes, concepts, or skills within the unit and across content areas are clearly identified.

  Example: A study of whole number operations with regard to money during math would be a parallel topic with a study of basic economics (goods and services) in a social studies unit.

- Overlapping themes, concepts, or skills with the unit and across content areas are clearly identified.

  Example: The use of charts and graphs to compare data might appear in math, science, and social studies content.

- Generalization of skills across content areas is reinforced.

OPPORTUNITIES TO PRACTICE SKILLS AND CONCEPTS (JUDICIOUS REVIEW: SUFFICIENT, DISTRIBUTED, VARIED, AND CUMULATIVE)

Review of key concepts and skills must be well planned and executed. Students with learning difficulties often have problems with retention and retrieval of information. In addition, many students with learning problems need a great deal of variety in order to stay task focused. When planning a unit of study, it is important to include planned opportunities to review previously learned concepts and skills on an ongoing and regular basis (Joint Committee on Teacher Planning for Students with Disabilities, 1995; Tomlinson, 1999; Burke et al., 1998).

- Daily opportunities to engage in a review of previously learned tool skills (skills necessary for completing higher level tasks such as capitalization, punctuation, basic math facts, or basic content area vocabulary content) are included in lesson plans.

- A variety of strategies are used to review content and skills (games, question-and-answer periods, application in cooperative learning activities, etc.).

- Major concepts and skills are reviewed periodically throughout the instructional unit.

- Skills reviewed over a weekly or biweekly timeframe reflect a cumulative informal assessment of the full scope and sequence previously taught.

Because we are busy, we sometimes forget to take time to look at the big picture. Even if we have students in our class who span several grade levels on achievement tests, we can still organize instruction around a manageable set of common objectives. During the elementary school years, students at each grade level learn about place value, whole number computation, time, measurement, problem-solving, money, fractions, and geometry in the math curriculum. Common science topics include space, plants, animals, ecology, simple machines, states of matter, and the scientific process. The study of health at each grade level addresses nutrition, growth and development, drug and alcohol awareness, and communicable diseases. Social studies topics tend to be more grade specific than other content but are easily integrated across grade levels with some attention to preplanning. The study of goods and services, colonial days, and state history are subtopics within social studies that can be taught simultaneously without losing essential concepts in any area. Language arts and reading skills are quite fluid from one grade level to the next. Punctuation, capitalization, spelling, and grammar as well as word attack skills and reading comprehension are easily integrated into all content area subjects. Sample lessons provided later in this chapter illustrate the integration of content across achievement levels.

Before beginning the planning cycle for an individual student, subgroup of students, or the whole class, however, check the county and state guidelines for each grade level. A hierarchy of skills across several grade levels in each content area can be of tremendous aid in the organization and integration of content across subject areas. This sounds more confusing as an abstract idea than it is when arranging real objectives. Think about one subject such as math. Place value, money, problem-solving, and whole number computation are taught in grades 1 through 6. Health and science content are often alternated. Suppose that for the portion of a grading period in which money and problem-solving were taught, the teacher decided to teach nutrition in health and economics in social studies. The overall theme for the unit might be titled: "Smart Shoppers and Healthy Choices." Take a look at the chart.

Exhibit 5-1. Sample Unit: Smart Shoppers and Healthy Choices

		Math	Science/Health	Social Studies	Reading	Language Arts
Grade 1		• Addition • Subtraction • Simple one step word problems • Coin value • Skip counting	• Food groups • Categorizing foods by group	• Community helpers	• Sight words • Decoding • Comprehension • Nonfiction: Detail/Facts • Fiction: Character Setting Problem Resolution	• Writing sentences • Spelling • Capitalization • End punctuation
Grade 2		• Addition, Subtraction of two digit numbers • Adding, Subtracting money values • One step word problems with and without distracters • Making change from $10	• Food groups • Categorizing foods by group • Number of servings and charting personal eating habits • Knowledge of nutrients found in each category of food	• Community helpers • Goods/Services • Natural resources • Manufactured goods	• Sight words • Decoding • Prefixes • Suffixes • Comprehension • Nonfiction: Detail/Facts • Main Idea	• Writing sentences and paragraphs • Spelling • Capitalization • End punctuation

	Math	Science/Health	Social Studies	Reading	Language Arts
Grade 3	• Addition, Subtraction of 3 digit numbers • Adding, Subtracting money values • One and two step word problems with and without distracters • Making change from $100	• Food groups • Categorizing foods by group • Number of servings and charting personal eating habits • Knowledge of nutrients found in each category of food	• Community helpers • Goods/Services • Natural resources • Manufactured goods	• Sight words • Decoding • Prefixes • Suffixes • Comprehension • Nonfiction: Detail/Facts Main Idea • Fiction: Character Setting Problem/ Resolution Cause/Effect Making Inferences	• Writing sentences and paragraphs • Spelling • Capitalization • End punctuation
Grade 4	• Addition • Subtraction • Division • Multiplication • One, two, and three step word problems with & without distracters • Making change from $1,000	• Food groups • Categorizing foods by group • Number of servings and charting personal eating habits • Knowledge of nutrients found in each category of food and disease preven- tion associated with each	• Community helpers • Goods/Services • Natural resources • Manufactured goods • Colonial life in a specified state compared with modern life	• Decoding • Prefixes • Suffixes • Comprehension • Nonfiction: Detail/Facts Main Idea Cause/Effect • Making Inferences • Fiction Character Setting Problem Resolution Cause/Effect Making Inferences	• Writing sentences, paragraphs, essays • Spelling • Capitalization • End punctuation

	Math	Science/Health	Social Studies	Reading	Language Arts
Grade 5	• Addition • Subtraction • Division • Multiplication • One, two, and three step word problems with & without distracters • Making change from $100,000	• Food groups • Categorizing foods by group • Number of servings and charting personal eating habits • Knowledge of nutrients found in each category of food and disease prevention associated with each as well as the organs in the body effected	• Community helpers • Goods/Services • Natural resources • Manufactured goods • Colonial life in the U.S.A. compared with modern life	• Decoding • Prefixes • Suffixes • Comprehension • Nonfiction: Detail/Facts Main Idea Cause/Effect • Making Inferences • Fiction: Character Setting Problem Resolution Cause/Effect	• Writing sentences, paragraphs, essays, reports • Spelling • Capitalization • End punctuation
Grade 6	• Addition • Subtraction • Division • Multiplication with whole numbers, per cents, and decimals • One, two and three step word problems, with and with out distracters • Making change from $1,000,000	• Food groups • Categorizing foods by group • Number of servings and charting personal eating habits • Knowledge of nutrients found in each category of food and disease preven--tion associated with each as well as the organs and systems in the body effected	• Community helpers • Goods/Services • Natural resources • Manufactured goods • Colonial life in the U.S.A. compared with conditions in other countries at the same period in history	• Decoding • Prefixes • Suffixes • Comprehension • Nonfiction: Detail/Facts Main Idea Cause/Effect Making Inferences • Fiction: Character Setting Problem Resolution	• Writing sentences, paragraphs, essays, reports, research projects • Spelling • Capitalization • End punctuation

Three major themes of the instructional unit as a whole might include:

1. How can I take responsibility for my health?

2. Which goods and services in the community help people to make healthy choices?

3. How can people use their talents and knowledge to help others in the community be healthy?

Each of the major themes can be developed at multiple levels across multiple content areas to meet the instructional needs of students. Books, poetry, newspaper articles, advertisements, movies, and materials from a variety of community agencies could be used as focal points for instruction. A teacher in a primary level class might use Jack Prelutsky (1984) poems such as "When Tillie Ate the Chili," "Baloney Belly Billy," and "When Mother Cooked The Turkey" to teach students to identify onsets and rhymes during reading, capitalization skills during language arts, food group categorization during health, and community helpers or goods and services during social studies. The poem "Baloney Belly Billy," describes a variety of items Billy would eat if given a penny, nickel, dime, half dollar, or quarter. Word problems could be developed related to information in the poem. A copy of the poem and sample lesson plan using the poem as a focal point for a variety of subject areas illustrates how to integrate multiple levels of academic achievement and student needs into one plan.

Exhibit 5-2. Baloney Belly Billy by Jack Prelutsky

*Baloney Belly Billy swallows anything for **cash**.*
*If you offer him a **penny**, he'll chew paper from the **trash**.*
*He'll eat guppies for a **nickel**. For a **dime**, he'll eat a **bug**.*
*And a **quarter** will convince him that he ought to eat a **slug**.*

*I have seen him eat a button. I have seen him eat a **bee**.*
*I have seen him eat three beetles for a half a dollar **fee**.*
*For a **dollar** he will gladly eat a lizard off the **fence**,*
*Just imagine what he'd swallow for another **fifty cents**!*

Exhibit 5-3. Multi-Level Lesson Plan
Shared Prompt: "Baloney Belly Billy" by Jack Prelutsky

Grade 1	Grade 2	Grade 3
Reading: • Identification of rhyming words and identification of sight words • Comprehension:Recall of detail	Reading: • Generation of word families based upon rhyming words in the poem Comprehension: • Recall of detail • Identification of character & setting	Reading Objectives: • Generation of word families based upon rhyming words in the poem & synonyms of targeted vocabulary Comprehension: • Recall of detail • Identification of setting, fact, fiction, and character
Math: • Identify words for coins, coin values, and coins themselves • Complete simple math problems related to poem content *Example:* How much would it cost to have Billy eat two guppies and a bug?	Math: • Identify words for coins, coin values, and coins themselves • Complete math problems related to poem content. Include distracters. *Example:* Billy eats 3 beetles for $.50, a bug for a dime and two guppies for a nickel. How much would it cost to have Billy eat two guppies and a bug?	Math: • Complete math problems related to poem content. • Generate change from $10.00 • Generate a chart that includes multiple combinations of coins for giving change of specified values.

Grade 1	Grade 2	Grade 3
Health: • Identify the items that Billy ate. • Categorize items according to items that are natural or man made. • Categorize pictures of foods according to the food group in which they belong	Health: • Identify the items that Billy ate. • Categorize items according to items that are natural or man made. • List the foods that they have eaten in a 24 hour period. • Categorize the foods according to the food group in which they belong. • Chart their results.	Health: • Identify the items that Billy ate. • Categorize items according to items that are natural or man made. • List the foods that they have eaten in a 24 hour period. • Categorize the foods according to the food group in which they belong. • Chart their results. • Compare their results to the suggested daily servings recommended by medical professionals.
Social Studies: • Identify the community helpers that Billy needs to see. • Build a miniature model town with a home for each student and a place of business for each student. • Label the community helpers represented in the places of business.	Social Studies: • Identify the community helpers, goods, and services that Billy needs to see. • Build a miniature model town with a home for each student and a place of business for each student. • Label the community helpers represented in the places of business.	Social Studies: • Identify the community helpers, goods, and services that Billy needs to see. • Build a miniature model town with a home for each student and a place of business for each student. • Label the community helpers represented in the places of business. • Develop a map of the streets, homes, and businesses for the miniature town.
Language Arts: • Write a sentence about your place of business and a sentence about your home. • Write a poem of your own using a fill-in-the-blank template developed using "Baloney Belly Billy" as a model.	Language Arts: • Write a paragraph about your place of business. • Write a poem of your own using a fill-in-the-blank template developed using "Baloney Belly Billy" as a model.	Language Arts: • Write 2 paragraphs about your place of business. • Write a poem of your own using a fill-in-the-blank template developed using "Baloney Belly Billy" as a model.

After organizing and aligning curriculum across skill and content areas, assess the oral comprehension level of the group. While a group of first, second, and third grade students may function academically at a level anywhere from pre-kindergarten to fourth grade, they will be able to function at the appropriate age level if the information is covered orally. Their ability levels in concept development and oral vocabulary comprehension will often be age appropriate despite lower reading and math achievement scores, unless their emotional problems include severe psychosis, autism, or mental disabilities.

Once the overall concept and vocabulary development of the group has been established, whole-group lessons can be taught orally at the appropriate grade level for their chronological ages. Written assignments can be adjusted for individual academic levels.

Once strategic integration of content has been established with attention to the individual as well as the group needs of the students, the selection of instructional supports becomes easier. Supports as defined by Carnine and Kameenui (1998) include: (a) clearly defining major concepts, (b) accessing prior knowledge, (c) teaching conspicuous strategies, (d) providing temporary supports, and (e) reviewing critical skills. Examples of each within each content area provide further application of the critical components of effective teaching.

MATH

Conventional math instruction is characterized by two phases. In the first phase, the teacher would demonstrate the process for completing a problem while students observed. Teachers typically demonstrated only one to four examples. The students were not actively engaged in asking questions or discussion. Following this passive student phase, independent work would be assigned. Teacher monitoring and feedback was typically inconsistent. This model of instruction is ineffective for the majority of students. Those with diverse learning needs are unable to acquire the skills and concepts necessary without active participation in instruction, guided practice with teacher mediated scaffolding, frequent monitoring to prevent repetitive practice of mistakes, corrective as well as positive feedback, and direct instruction in self-monitoring strategies. Dixon, Carnine, Lee, Wallin, & Chard (1998) describe a three-phase process for effective instruction that facilitates skill and concept mastery.

> **Phase 1** Teachers demonstrate, explain, and engage students in a discussion about the concept or skill. Definitions, critical attributes, examples, nonexamples, and sequences or patterns are fully developed through interactive questioning and discussion with students. Students are actively engaged.

> **Phase 2** Teachers provide additional examples of the concept or skill for students to work through with assistance. During the guided practice phase, students are provided with teacher mediated scaffolding in the forms of charts, calculators, peer buddies with advanced skills, and other learning aids. Teachers monitor students' progress and provide frequent corrective feedback. Teacher-mediated support is gradually faded as students demonstrate mastery.

Phase 3 Teachers assess students' mastery levels in basic skills and in students' abilities to apply skills and concepts to problem solving. Students demonstrate their abilities to independently recall basic facts and to generalize or transfer their knowledge to new problem-solving tasks.

In addition to utilizing effective instructional formats, adequate time for mastering each new concept or skill and the sequencing of skills need to be carefully considered. Students with recall deficits benefit from repetition. Sequencing the order of skill instruction to ensure that each skill builds a foundation for the next skill and that no skill is ever entirely dropped from the instructional content is helpful. This can be achieved by having students complete brief daily drills of 5-10 problems representative of previously mastered problems while waiting for the teacher to take attendance.

Word problems require specific skills of organization and evaluation no matter how easy or difficult the final computation may be. Select a word problem to work together orally that will employ skills each member of the group is using in independent work. Read the problem aloud. Then guide the group through the following activities:

1. Ask, "What information do we need to solve this problem?"

2. Ask, "What operation will we use?" Give each student an opportunity to respond to this question. Put a +, -, x, or ÷ sign next to each person's name as he or she responds. Allow divergent answers and discussion of reasons each student has for his or her answer.

3. Ask the students for ideas on how to illustrate the problem. Have appropriate pictures or manipulatives available.

4. After illustrations are complete and correct based on the information in the problem, ask once again whether the students are satisfied with their choice of operation. Make changes based on their responses.

5. Ask, "Does this answer make sense? Does the answer match our illustration?"

Use this daily oral problem-solving practice as a springboard for specific skill development. One student may be learning place value through the millions, another through hundreds, and another through tens. They will all benefit from a group discussion process. The more advanced students gain confidence from assisting others. The less advanced students begin to understand how what they are learning builds on other ideas. They begin to feel more capable as they realize that they are using the same manipulatives as more advanced students and can indeed hold their own in the group process. The teacher can create an atmosphere of respect for each student's abilities by structuring the questioning to include each person at his or her level of competence. A problem-solving map can also be used during guided and independent practice to assist students in thinking about the process. An example is provided on the next page.

Exhibit 5-4. Word Problem Map

What is the goal of the problem?	Jose wanted to tile his bedroom floor. His bedroom is 10' x 12'. The tiles are 12" x 12" and cost $5.00 each. Jose has $650.00. How much will he have left after he buys the tile? *Goal:* The amount of money Jose has left after he buys tile for his bedroom.
Draw a picture to illustrate the problem.	
Select the necessary information.	120 tiles $5.00 each Jose has $650.00
Decide operation(s).	Multiply 120 x $5.00 Subtract the product from $650.0
Compute Add, Subtract, Multiply, Divide	120 x $5.00 = $600.00 $650.00 - $600.00 = $50.0

A mini-test given each day on facts related to each student's skill level is another way to involve the whole group while meeting individual needs. Divide addition, subtraction, multiplication, and division facts into 20-item mini-tests. Other information can be divided in a similar fashion. Measurement tables and area and perimeter formulas can be made into mini-tests. Each student is given a mini-test each day. The timer is set for 1 minute. When students score 90% or better on their mini-test, they mark their progress on a chart. Mastery of all addition facts or subtraction facts will earn the student a special reward of some kind. It is not necessary to set a time limit for mastery. Students compete against themselves—no one else. Extra practice on items not mastered can be provided as homework and during independent work times.

Materials needed for whole-group problem-solving include a resource for daily word problems related to the group's needs, manipulatives, and a chalkboard or overhead projector. Mini-tests are drawn from multiple copies of facts tests based on individual skill levels, a timer, progress charts for each student, and follow-up activities for reinforcement.

Using this lesson format, a typical 45-minute math period would be conducted as follows:
- 15 minutes for oral whole-group problem solving.
- 5 minutes for the mini-test and scoring.
- 15 minutes for guided practice on a new or developing skill. (During this time, students can be grouped for targeted instruction. A classroom assistant or adult volunteer can help with a smaller skill group.)
- 10 minutes for independent practice.

Be sure to use hands-on, manipulative materials when introducing a new concept or skill. Move to pictorial representations (charts, drawings, or photographs) only after students fully understand the material. Allow students to continue to use pictorial representations until they are able to complete a problem of a particular type abstractly.

READING/SCIENCE/SOCIAL STUDIES

Vocabulary development and comprehension skills can be taught orally at the group's overall oral comprehension level. Multiple meanings of words, prefixes, suffixes, sequencing, characterization, and other elements of literature can be presented to the whole group through discussion and listening activities. In the area of science and social studies concept development, enrichment activities such as experiments, construction projects, and field trips can provide ample whole-group instructional time.

Read a selection, show a movie, or show a filmstrip to introduce information to the whole group. Follow this with discussions and questions designed to instruct and reinforce. To test understanding, provide skill worksheets at individual reading levels. Testing can be done with the whole group at once by giving the students oral questions with written answers. Written answers can be words taken from a word bank written on the chalkboard, true or false, happy face or sad face, or a code of some kind—perhaps having the students write the first letter of key words while statements are read or use geometric symbols to represent certain words or concepts. For instance, after studying systems of the body, students might write a D for digestive system, a C for circulatory system, or an N for nervous system as the teacher reads functions and representative organs.

Additional strategies for assisting students in organizing information are provided on the following pages.

CONCEPT MAPS

Concept maps can be used to informally assess students' prior knowledge and assist them in understanding how previously mastered skills and concepts relate to a new unit of study (Hyerle, 1996; Boudah, Lenz, Bulgren, Schumaker, & Deshler, 2000; Deshler, Ellis, & Lenz, 1996). Different concept maps illustrate relationships among topics and subtopics of specific types. The five types of concept maps included in this section are as follows:

1. Concept webs used to illustrate subtopics that are related and are of equal status or value.
2. Hierarchical charts used to illustrate relationships among subtopics that are of unequal value or status.
3. Cyclical charts used to illustrate repetitive steps or stages.
4. Flow charts used illustrate sequential steps or stages.
5. Venn diagrams used to compare and contrast two or more subtopics or concepts.

The **Concept Web** can be used to illustrate relationships among subtopics and the main idea.

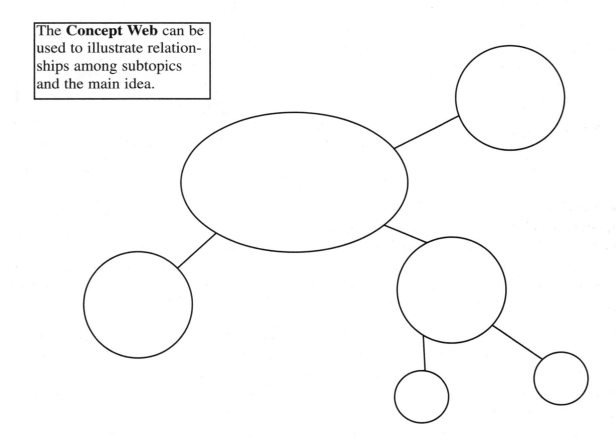

Concept webs are used to illustrate subtopics that are related and are of equal status or value. An example of this type of information would be the subtopics under the main heading of a particular culture. The culture would be written in the large oval. Foods, art, shelter and other subtopics would be written in the medium-sized circles. Individual details about foods, art, and shelter would be written in the small circles connected to the medium-sized circles.

The Hierarchical Chart could be used to illustrate branches of the government in social studies, the taxonomy of living organisms is science, or the organization of main ideas and supporting details in a nonfiction reading selection.

The **Hierarchical Chart** can be used to illustrate relationships among subtopics that are aligned consistent-

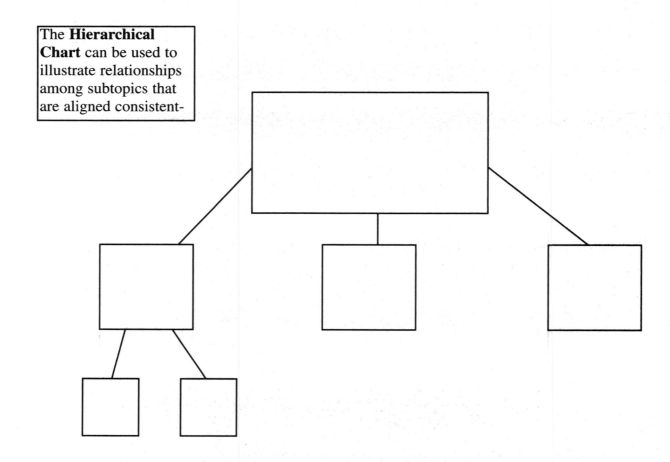

The Cyclical Chart is useful in illustrating stages in the life cycle of insects, the water cycle, and cause-and-effect relationships in fiction as well as nonfiction reading selections.

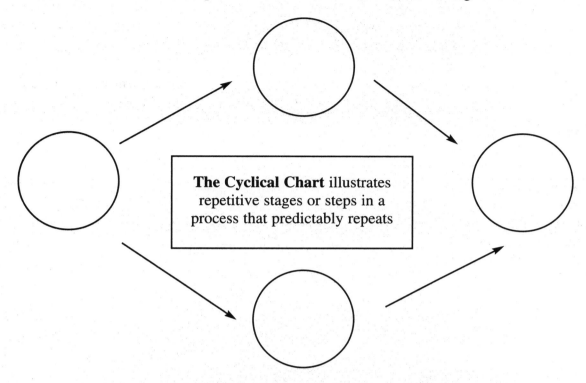

The Flow Chart is useful in illustrating sequential steps for completing any task. Applications could include computation problems requiring multiple steps, the analysis of word problems, recipes, craft projects, accessing and storing instructional materials, entering the room after lunch or enrichment classes, and preparing to leave in the afternoon.

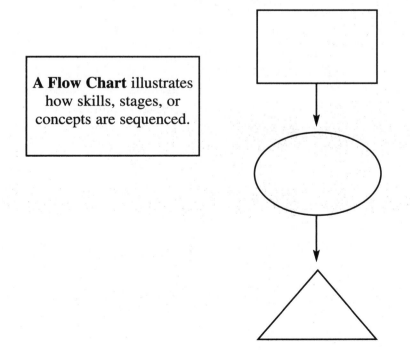

The Venn Diagram is useful in assisting students with connections between previously mastered concepts and new concepts. Critical differences between two concepts can be written on the far left and far right sections of the diagram. Shared attributes can be written in the middle of the diagram. During lessons in algebraic thinking, students can be challenged to compare and contrast properties such as commutative and associative. For younger students, drawings and photographs can be used along with words to assist them in understanding and remembering the information presented.

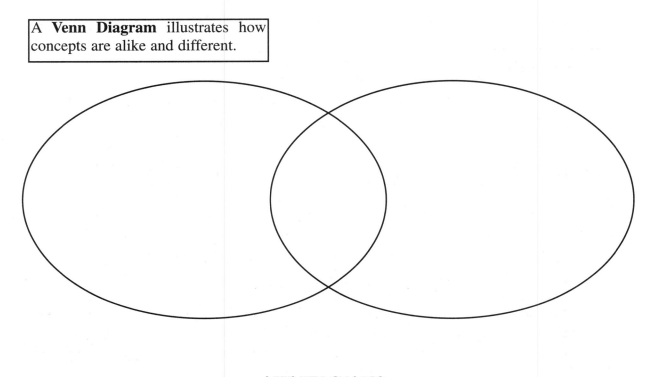

A **Venn Diagram** illustrates how concepts are alike and different.

AFFINITY CHARTS

Affinity charts are a useful tool to use during informal assessment of prior knowledge as well as during instructional activities aimed at linking prior knowledge with new content (McClanahan & Wicks, 1993). The easiest way to develop an affinity chart with large groups of students is to provide individuals, partners, or small groups with several blank 3"x5" index cards and ask them to write one fact about a designated topic on each card. Placing students with diverse needs in small groups with typically achieving students facilitates discussion and tends to broaden the range of responses generated. After students have had time to write responses on the cards provided, ask each individual or group to read their responses and tape them to a bulletin board or wall. As each group makes their presentation, duplicate facts can be omitted. The cards on the bulletin board or wall will be arranged randomly. Ask students to look at the facts on each card and identify subtopics suggested by the facts. Make subtopic headings and have students assist in arranging the facts under their appropriate category headings. This student-generated chart can then be used as a reference point for introducing new information related to the overall topic and to the appropriate subtopics as instruction progresses from day to day.

Step 1. Identify the topic and ask students to write facts about the topic on 3"x5" index cards.

Step 2. Place all responses on a bulletin board or wall.

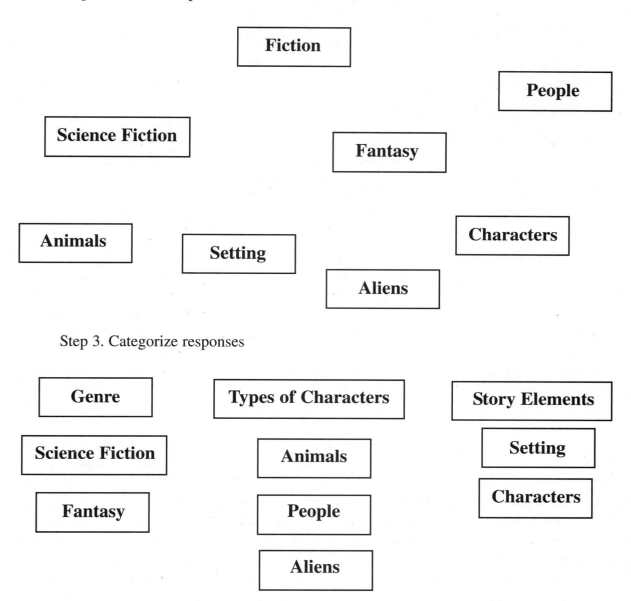

Step 3. Categorize responses

Step 4. Use the items that the students generated to introduce new information about fiction such as additional genres, story elements, authors.

ANALOGIES

Students incorporate new information more efficiently if they are able to make connections between prior understandings and novel concepts (Deshler & Schumaker, 1986; Deshler, Ellis, & Lenz, 1996). When introducing new vocabulary or topics of interest, it is often effective to begin with a concept that is already well understood. For example, one teacher wanted students to understand the purpose and processes necessary for effectively engaging in cooperative learning. To introduce the concept of cooperative learning, the teacher began by having students generate a list of teams that they had watched or been a member of. These team names were listed on the board. Students were then asked to list the attributes of an effective (good) team player. The students responded with (a) takes turns, (b) helps others, (c) completes tasks, (d) listens to the coach, and other admirable characteristics of a valuable team player. The teacher then defined cooperative learning as a team approach to mastering academic skills and concepts. Students were able to understand and utilize the information about effective cooperative learning after making an analogy to team participation.

Venn diagrams and concept maps are additional ways to illustrate analogies while assisting students in making connections between previously mastered concepts and new content. Another graphic organizer that can be useful during the exploration of analogies is the concept attribute chart. This chart includes spaces along the left vertical margin for concepts targeted for comparison. Along the top horizontal margin, attributes of one or all of the targeted concepts are listed. Students place a mark under each attribute that is true for each concept. The resulting chart provides an illustration of likes and differences among targeted concepts as shown in the example on the next page.

Exhibits 5-5. Pretests

	True Story	Make-Believe	Main Ideals About A Person's Life	Story Is About the Author	Includes Animals & Plants That Talk
Biography	X		X		
Autobiography	X		X	X	
Realistic Fiction		X			

Pretests are as important informal assessments for teachers to consider (Hall, 2002c). The analysis of pretests allows the teacher to plan more effectively for instruction. Time is not spent on information that students have already mastered. Skill groups can be established early in a unit to facilitate mastery of targeted concepts. In addition to providing valuable instructional information for the teacher, however, pretests cue students about the important concepts in a new lesson or unit and help students begin to link prior knowledge with new material. Some textbooks provide pretests for use before each new unit of study. If the pretests are appropriate for all students in the class and meet state and local standards for instruction, it is wise to use them regularly. If the curriculum materials in use do not include pretests, consider using one or more of the instructional strategies outlined in this section on activating prior knowledge as a pretest. These strategies will provide information about students' strengths and needs as a group while cuing students on important information and skills that will be included in the coming unit. In addition, the use of charts and other graphic organizers will assist students with diverse needs in organizing new material and developing their own cognitive maps for greater retention and retrieval of information.

VOCABULARY AND CONCEPT DEVELOPMENT AND COMPREHENSION

Flow Charts and other graphic organizers were introduced in the section on activating prior knowledge. These same tools are also representative of conspicuous strategies that individuals who have reached mastery in a particular skill area utilize informally. When planning to teach a new concept or skill, select the most appropriate graphic organizer for the content and plan to teach the strategy along with the targeted content. Additional strategies not addressed previously include rubrics and mnemonic strategies. Both are described on the following pages.

Rubrics are effective tools for students with diverse needs to use in learning to self-evaluate. As stated earlier, students with diverse needs often have difficulty knowing what they do well and what they need additional help mastering. This deficit in self-knowledge makes it difficult for them to organize, prioritize, and efficiently utilize resources. Rubrics can be of tremendous assistance in helping these students gain the self-knowledge they need to reach higher levels of achievement (Andrade, 2000).

Before beginning a project, book report, or some other assignment that includes a finished product, engage students in the development of a rubric. To help them understand how to construct and use a rubric, start with a simple cooking or craft activity. One group made a simple candy recipe that required no cooking. Students mixed the ingredients, rolled them into bite-sized balls, and dusted them with powdered sugar. When they completed the task, they were asked what they would want to see in such a product if they were asked to pay for them before eating them. Students generated a list of desired attributes and put one attribute on each blank index card provided. After generating the list of attributes, they categorized them by qualities related to taste, size, shape, and texture. These attributes formed the highest possible level on their rubric. From that level they described characteristics of the worst candy possible for the lowest level on the rubric. Once the best and worst were identified, they described two intermediate levels between the best and worst. The teacher then asked the students to rate the candy they had made according to the rubric. They placed candy representing each level on four different plates with descriptors for the designated level next to the plate. Another class completed a similar process by making simple pom pom and pipe cleaner pencil pals. While it is not essential that students begin their understanding of rubrics with a "fun" activity, such activities do motivate students who are reluctant to engage in academic tasks.

The following rubric for scoring projects was developed by students and used during peer and teacher feedback sessions. Models from previous groups were reviewed prior to beginning projects. Students had an opportunity to help rate those projects with the former students' names removed. This activity makes expectations explicit for students who may not be able to understand the more subtle or implicit components of quality work production.

An additional rubric describing quality team work was also constructed by a group of students. This rubric was used daily during individual and group evaluation periods. Using rubrics for academic and behavioral evaluation can strengthen the effectiveness of cooperative learning activities in the areas of achievement and conduct.

Exhibit 5-6. Rubric for Scoring Projects

	Content	Illustrations	Format	Mechanics
4	Additional information provided Difficult subject or topic	Photographs Samples	3-D Display Organization highlighted with colors &/or different types of font	Correct spelling, capitalization, and punctuation as well as the use of a higher level of vocabulary, formulas, or report construction
3	All required sections completed	Data graphed Hand drawn pictures	Placed on a poster in an organized fashion	Correct spelling, Capitalization, and punctuation
2	60% or more of the content included	Data included, but not graphed	Placed on notebook paper Disorganized Not labeled properly	A few mistakes with spelling, capitalization, and punctuation
1	Less than 60% of the content included	Incomplete data	Written entirely in pencil Messy Difficult to read	

Exhibit 5-7. Quality Teamwork

	0	**1**	**2**	**3**
• *Ready on time*	No one ready	A few ready	Most ready	All ready
• *Listen during lesson*	No one listening	A few listening	Most listening	All listening
• *Work quietly*	No one on task	A few on task	Most on task	All on task & quiet
• *Complete work*	No one done	A few done	Most done	All work done
• *Clean area*	Area messy	A few in place	Most in place	All in place

Mnemonics are memory strategies that can be quite helpful for students who have difficulty with retention and retrieval of basic facts (Carney, Levin, & Levin, 1993). The following strategies can be easily incorporated into lesson planning and implementation. Once students understand the usefulness of the strategies, they can be challenged to develop their own mnemonic devices.

1. Visual chains are like flow charts or cyclical graphic organizers but include pictures, icon, or symbols and use as few words as possible (Chan, Cole, & Morris, 1990; Carney, Levin, & Levin, 1993; Frender, 1990; Deshler, Ellis, & Lenz, 1996).

2. Acronyms are words such as ROY G BIV that assist in the memorization and/or order of targeted information. ROY G BIV stands for the order of the colors in the spectrum—Red, Orange, Yellow, Green, Blue, Indigo, and Violet. The first letter of each word targeted for memorization is a letter required for spelling the acronym (Chan, Cole, & Morris, 1990; Carney, Levin, & Levin, 1993; Frender, 1990; Deshler, Ellis, & Lenz, 1996).

3. Poems, rhymes, lyrics, or nonsense verses can also be used as memory aids. Most students are familiar with the ABC song. Another example is the poem about the number of days in each month (Chan, Cole, & Morris, 1990; Carney, Levin, & Levin, 1993; Frender, 1990; Deshler, Ellis, & Lenz, 1996).

4. Acrostics are similar to acronyms. The difference is that the first letter of each word in an acrostic sentence represents the first letter in the targeted information such as King Philip Came Over For Green Soup which stands for kingdom, phylum, class, order, family, genus, species (Chan, Cole, & Morris, 1990; Carney, Levin, & Levin, 1993; Frender, 1990; Deshler, Ellis, & Lenz, 1996).

5. Tape recordings can also be made. Some students remember information that they hear repeatedly more efficiently than information they read repeatedly (Chan, Cole, & Morris, 1990; Carney, Levin, & Levin, 1993; Frender, 1990; Deshler, Ellis, & Lenz, 1996).

6. Mental pictures linked to real objects can also be helpful. Students can remember prepositions by placing objects in relation to each other as an illustration and then visualizing the objects and actions later (Chan, Cole, & Morris, 1990; Carney, Levin, & Levin, 1993; Frender, 1990; Deshler, Ellis, & Lenz, 1996).

7. Graphic organizers described in the section on activating prior knowledge are also helpful in strengthening students' retention of information (Chan, Cole, & Morris, 1990; Carney, Levin, & Levin, 1993; Frender, 1990; Deshler, Ellis, & Lenz, 1996; Hyerle, 1996).

Agendas—One of the primary characteristics of students with diverse needs is their inability to organize and prioritize materials, time, concepts, and assignments. Educators can teach students to organize and prioritize tasks and resources by (a) modeling these metacognitive skills through the posting of daily and monthly schedules; (b) reviewing the posted agendas frequently throughout the days, weeks, and months; (c) and teaching students to utilize their own personal agendas.

Pictures and drawings can be used to illustrate routine assignments and events for younger students who are still learning to read or older students who require nonverbal cues due to emerging reading skills. In the beginning, students can be given a daily agenda with routine information and events such as times for specific content lessons, lunch and outside enrichment classes already completed for them. Students can be asked to complete special information on the daily agenda during opening discussions in the morning. As the day progresses, students can be asked to check items completed and rate themselves on their level of mastery in meeting time goals for task completion.

As students gain more skills in reading and following an agenda, less information should be preprinted on the agenda. Students can be expected to complete more complex weekly or monthly agendas as well. Examples of daily and weekly agenda and goal sheets are provided at the end of the section on goal sheets.

Goal Sheets are similar to agendas, but may include only one academic area or specific skill at a time and should be more individualized. For example, if the agenda for the week includes preparing an oral book report for presentation on Friday, a student's individual goal sheet would include steps the student plans to take in order to complete his or her presentation. All students might be required to submit an outline that includes the title, author, setting, characters, conflict or problem, major events leading to and resolving the problem, and the resolution. Construction of the outline would be a common feature on all students' goal sheets. Methods of presentation may vary, however, from student to student. One student might choose to dress as the main character in the book, another might construct a model of the setting, a third student might use a flannel board or puppet show to describe a main event in the book. Methods of presentation, props required, as well as materials and timelines for completion would vary from individual to individual.

Students can begin to complete goal sheets for specific time-limited activities in the primary grades as a strategy for teaching students to plan and increasing their motivation to take ownership of their learning processes. Older students may also need experiences with specific time-limited goal sheet completion prior to being expected to complete and follow more complex goal setting routines. Examples of agendas and goal sheets that can be gradually constructed with increasing levels of abstraction and student ownership are provided below and on the following pages.

Exhibit 5-8. Today's Agenda

Name _____   Date_____

Time	Activities	How I Did
8:30-9:30	Reading	
9:30-10:30	Math	
10:30-11:30	Science	
11:00-11:30 (Insert One)	Art Computer Lab Music	
11:30-12:00	Lunch	

Name _____   Date_____

Time	Activities	How I Did
		_____
8:30-9:30	Reading	_____
9:30-10:30	Math	_____
10:30-11:30	Science	_____
11:00-11:30 (Insert One)	Fill in the Blank	_____
11:30-12:00	Lunch	

This Work Sign-off Sheet can be used as an agenda and goal sheet in one. Target Behaviors can be selected by the students and include social skills, classroom conduct, completion of classwork or homework on time, completion of a checkpoint on a long-term assignment, targeted skill mastery level, or any combination of the above. These work sign-off sheets can be taped to each student's desk and provide a running record of progress for the week. Students can write grades earned on assignments, check marks, or some other form of documentation and take the sheets home on Fridays to share with parents.

Exhibit 5-9. Work Sign-off Sheet

Name _____ **Week of** _____

	Monday	Tuesday	Wednesday	Thursday	Friday
DOL/WOD					
Reading					
Language					
Spelling					
Math					
Science/Soc. St.					
Homework					

Target Behaviors

A.

B.

C.

D.

For older, more academically capable students, the agenda and time management documentation can be included on the same chart. Each student would be responsible for completing the daily agenda for a specific subject area and establishing time goals for work completion. The students record their progress on the assignments in the small rectangular box to the right of the day's agenda and their time management achievement level on the chart at the top of the column for the current week. Time management points would be approximations based on task completion. If half of the day's agenda was completed, the chart would reflect 50 points in that area—one fourth of the day's agenda would be reflected with 25 points—all of the day's agenda would be reflected with 100 points. Students with diverse learning needs benefit from daily, graphic reminders of their progress.

Intermediate checkpoints should be included on assignment sheets, agendas, and goal sheets. The need for frequent intermediate checkpoints will vary from student to student. Some students will be successful with a description of an assignment and a due date. Other students will only need to have the planning stages of a project or assignment checked for accuracy and thoroughness. Other students will require intermediate due dates for planning, rough drafts, editing, and final drafts. The frequency of checkpoints can be gradually faded as students demonstrate mastery in organization and prioritization of task completion with regard to time, materials, and other resources.

Exhibit 5-10. Book Report Checklist
(for beginners or those with organizational challenges)

Name _____   Date _____

Due Date(s)

_____ 1. Select a fiction book and gather signatures.
       Book Title _____
       Author's Name _____
       Parent's Signature _____
       Teacher's Signature _____

_____ 2. Read the first half if the book and record the following
              information:
       Type of Fiction _____
       Setting _____
       Characters _____
       Problem/Conflict _____

_____ 3. Read the second half of the book and record the following
              information:
       Action 1 _____
       Action 2 _____
       Action 3 _____
       Resolution _____

_____ 4. Write a rough draft of the report.

_____ 5. Edit the report with a Study Buddy._____
                           (Study Buddy's Signature)

_____ 6. Submit final draft of the report.

Book Report Checklist
(for intermediate level organizers)

Name _____   Date _____

Due Date(s)

_____   1. Select a fiction book and gather signatures.
          Book Title _____
          Author's Name _____
          Parent's Signature _____
          Teacher's Signature _____

_____   2. Read the book and record the following information:
          Type of Fiction _____
          Setting _____
          Characters _____
          Problem/Conflict _____
          Action 1 _____
          Action 2 _____
          Action 3 _____
          Resolution _____

_____   3. Write a rough draft of the report.

_____   4. Edit the report with a Study Buddy._____
                                        (Study Buddy's Signature)

_____   5. Submit final draft of the report.

Book Report Checklist
(for mastery level organizers)

Name _____   Date _____

Due Date(s)
_____ 1. Select a fiction book and gather signatures.
            Book Title _____
            Author's Name _____
            Parent's Signature _____
            Teacher's Signature _____

_____ 2. Edit the rough draft of the report with a Study Buddy.
            _____
            (Study Buddy's Signature)

_____ 3. Submit final draft of the report.

Cognitive Credit Cards (Edmunds, 1999) are another strategy that can be effective with students who have diverse learning needs. Like the agendas, goal sheets, and intermediate checkpoint sheets described above, cognitive credit cards can be developed with students and contain fewer prompts as students reach higher levels of mastery. The cognitive credit card is a 3" by 5" index card with cues or prompts that can be used when a student is unsure of how to proceed with a task. During direct instruction, students might be encouraged to try a number of strategies when they come to an unfamiliar word in a reading assignment. These strategies might include (a) examining the onset and rhymes in the word for familiar patterns, (b) looking for prefixes and suffixes that might provide clues, (c) thinking about the context of the sentence or paragraph, and (d) looking for the word in the glossary or a dictionary. To assist students in remembering the steps to follow when they find an unfamiliar word, the teacher can guide the students in developing a cognitive credit card with the steps printed on it. Students keep the credit card handy during all reading assignments including content area and recreational reading. The cognitive credit cards can be reconstructed over time with fewer prompts as students master the skills for which the card was developed. Cognitive credit cards are beneficial for the following reasons:

1. They are easy to individualize.
2. They can be adjusted to meet the needs of students as their levels of
   mastery increase.
3. They allow students to be more independent.
4. They assist students in feeling more self-confident.

The following set of cognitive credit cards for students with increasing levels of mastery illustrate the flexibility and potential benefit of incorporating this strategy into ongoing instructional routines.

Exhibit 5-11. Cognitive Credit Cards

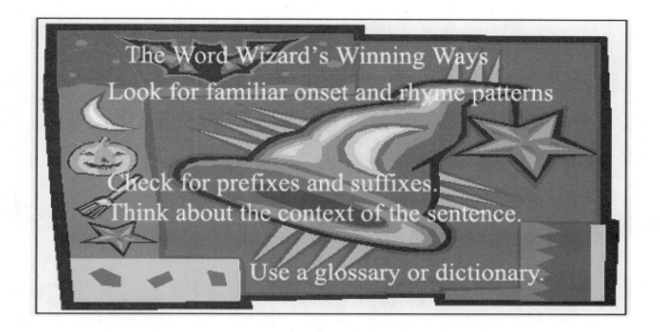

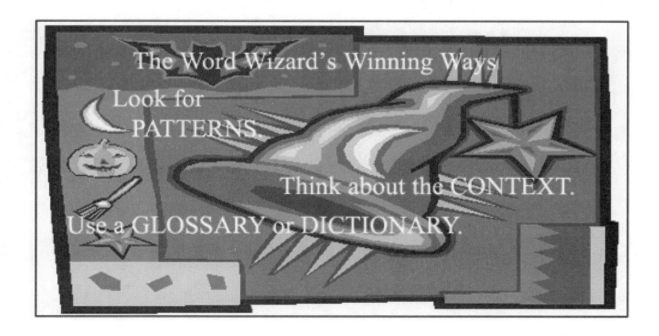

Outlining and note taking routines can also be constructed to allow for gradual fading of prompts. In the beginning, students can be provided with outlines or notes that are complete and be instructed to highlight key information as it is discussed or read. Once students are proficient in identifying key information on the outlines or notes, they can be given outlines or notes with blanks to complete as they read. The next step in process of mediated scaffolding for outlining and note taking would include cues about the number of items (supporting details) to locate under subtopics. The final step would be to simply assign outlining or note taking as part of the learning tasks for a unit of study. An example is provided below of the levels of scaffolding that might be useful within a given group of students.

Exhibit 5-12. Example of Levels of Scaffolding

Vertebrates

    I. Reptiles
        A. Have dry, scaly skin
        B. Are cold blooded
   II. Amphibians
        A. Live a double life
        B. Have gills when young and lungs as adults
  III. Birds
        A. Have feathers
        B. Lay eggs
   IV. Fish
        A. Have gills
        B. Have scales
    V. Mammals
        A. Have hair or fur
        B. Feed their babies milk

Vertebrates

I. Reptiles
    A. Have _____ skin
    B. Are _____ blooded
II. Amphibians
    A. Live a _____ life
    B. Have _____ when young and _____ as adults
III. Birds
    A. Have _____ for an outer covering
    B. Lay _____

IV. Fish
    A. Have _____ for breathing
    B. Have _____ for an outer covering
V. Mammals
    A. Have _____ or _____ for an outer covering
    B. Feed their babies _____

Vertebrates

I. Reptiles
    A.
    B.
II. Amphibians
    A.
    B.
III. Birds
    A.
    B.
IV. Fish
    A.
    B.
V. Mammals
    A.
    B.

CHOICES IN ACCESSING INFORMATION

Students with diverse needs benefit from utilizing multiple sources of information and have choices about the sources of information they access during selected assignments and activities (Deshler, Ellis, & Lenz, 1996). Students who read fluently and exhibit high levels of achievement in reading comprehension are able to access information through traditional textbook assignments. Students with diverse learning needs, however, often exhibit learning strengths in areas that are not traditionally available in a textbook driven environment. Researchers have found that students who are able to access information in their area of strength for at least a part of their academic work time experience higher rates of academic achievement than those who are required to access information in their areas of weakness alone.. The following list of choices for accessing information should be made available to students when the lesson objectives and resources available permit.

1. Highlight key concepts is a selected and coded set of content area textbooks. Students with diverse needs can be given the previously highlighted textbooks to help them locate and focus on important information in the text. Highlighted areas should be completely outlined in color in the beginning and can even be color coded by category (key words, main ideas, supporting details). About a third of the way through the textbook, highlighted areas can be reduced to include key words and main ideas only. By the end of the book, a note at the beginning of the chapter to locate key words, main ideas, and supporting details for recording in a notebook might be all that is necessary for continued success. The highlighted textbook helps students become aware of how to separate essential from non-essential information and structure their reading and study time.

2. Establish listening centers in the classroom with textbooks recorded on audio-tapes. Students who do not need to listen to the text in order to understand and retain information will not use the listening centers once the novelty has faded. Making the listening centers available to all students, however, reduces the stigma students with diverse needs might feel if they were assigned to use the listening centers exclusively.

3. Make content-related videos and documentaries available to students. Some students might remember more from a listening center. Other students might remember more after seeing and hearing a video. Allowing students to select among two or three choices empowers and motivates them.

4. Provide a variety of reading materials such as Newspapers, Magazines, and Illustrated Reference Books. Many illustrated books contain as much information as a text without pictures, but the illustrated information is more accessible to students with visual strengths.

5. Make computer and internet resources available to students as often as possible. CAST at www.cast.org has information on software that can make any digital text accessible to students with diverse needs. Through their eReader software, students can enlarge print, highlight key information, use a split screen to take notes while reading text, and even have the text read aloud. In addition, information can be located on the internet at various reading levels, making content assessable to groups that have a wide range of reading skills.

6. Make resources with a wide range of reading levels available to all students.

7. Include interviews, quest speakers, community resources, and field trips in the list of resources used to develop a unit.

CHOICES IN DEMONSTRATING MASTERY

Students with diverse needs benefit from opportunities to use multiple methods when demonstrating mastery and have choices about the methods they use as outcome measures for selected assignments and activities. Students who read fluently and exhibit high levels of achievement in reading comprehension are able to access information through traditional textbook assignments and demonstrate mastery of content by answering traditional textbook questions. Students with diverse learning needs, however, often exhibit learning strengths in areas that are not traditionally demonstrated in a textbook driven environment. Researchers have found that students who are able to demonstrate mastery of content using their area of strength for at least a part of their academic work experience higher rates of academic achievement than those who are required to demonstrate mastery of content through their areas of weakness alone. The following list of choices for demonstrating mastery should be made available to students when the lesson objectives and resources available permit.

1. Use written and oral testing procedures.

2. Allow students to illustrate concepts with drawings or graphs, build models, or take photographs to demonstrate mastery of key concepts.

3. Engage students in developing demonstrations for the class or other groups.

4. Encourage students to document growth and mastery through the development of a video or portfolio.

5. Allow students to include any of the items listed in 2, 3, or 4 as support materials when writing a more traditional research paper.

COOPERATIVE LEARNING

Key elements of cooperative learning are beneficial to students with diverse needs (Hall, 2002b) and lend themselves to mediated scaffolding through teacher planning. The key elements related to mediated scaffolding are listed below.

1. Group students with complementary strengths—one who writes and spells well, one who reads well, one with artistic ability, and one with a relative strength in math.

2. Describe the roles that group members will take and assist groups in selecting the most appropriate member for the role—scribe, time keeper, illustrator, interpreter of directions, etc.

3. Provide a structure for students to use in evaluating their behavioral as well as their academic performance. Student-generated rubrics (explained in the section on conspicuous strategies) are an effective method for assisting students in self and group evaluation.

4. Develop cooperative learning activities and tasks that require the group to work together, but also include individual accountability. An example of a task that requires group interaction and individual accountability is described as follows. After a unit on writing persuasive essays, each cooperative learning group is given a product and told that they must write a 5-10 minute infomercial script designed to sell the product. The group will perform the informercial skit complete with props. The group must submit an infomercial plan that includes the names of the prop design chairperson, the director, the actors and their roles, and the time keeper. The infomercial plan should also include a brief summary of the skit. Individuals will be held accountable for their performances as well as for their part in developing the skit (props, script, organization, etc.). In addition, each group member will be required to compose a three to five paragraph persuasive essay based on the skit after the performance.

Students with diverse needs benefit from the group discussions about the assigned topic, have an active role as a group participant, are provided opportunities to demonstrate related strengths and talents, and are still held accountable individually for the targeted academic content.

Website addresses with additional information on cooperative learning, peer tutoring, and other effective methods of peer mediated instruction are included below.

- Jigsaw Classroom   http://jigsaw.org
- Office of Research, Education Consumer Guides: Cooperative Learning
  http://www.ed.gov/pubs/OR/ConsumerGuides/cooplear.html
- Peer Tutoring and Cross-Age Tutoring
  http://www.nwrel.org/scpd/sirs/9/c018.html

• The Effects of Instructional Grouping Format on the Reading Outcomes of Students with Disabilities: A Meta-Analytic Review
http://ncld.org/research/osep_reading.cfm

SUFFICIENT OPPORTUNITIES FOR REVIEW

1. Brief daily reviews such as Word of the Day, Daily Oral Language, and Bell Drills can be used to assist students in focusing their attention on academic content upon entering the classroom in the morning, after lunch, and after outside enrichment classes (Deshler, Ellis, & Lenz, 1996).

Word of the Day—Select key vocabulary based on current academic content.Write one word on the board each day. Students record the word in a word bank, define it, write a sentence using the word, and/or draw a picture to illustrate the meaning of the word. Words that might be selected for Word of the Day include elements of fiction such as character and setting, elements of nonfiction such as main idea and supporting detail, or interesting adjectives such as dainty, enormous, and ferocious. Once a week, students can be tested on their knowledge of the meanings of previously learned words. Eight words from previous days can be listed on the board. The teacher provides the meanings orally for five of the eight words. The students write the words that correspond to the definitions on their paper.

Daily Oral Language—Write one or two sentences on the board each day that contain punctuation, capitalization, and/or grammar errors. Students write the sentences in a language journal and correct errors. During whole group instruction, students orally discuss the errors in the sentences on the board and check their own work.

Bell Drills—Provide students with brief one-to-three paragraph reading selections taken from curriculum materials, leveled library books, or youth magazines written at the appropriate reading level for the students in the class. These can be placed on an overhead transparency or distributed to students on half sheets of letter-sized paper. Ask students to answer three-to-five comprehension questions related to previously learned comprehension skills. To more effectively reinforce a particular comprehension skill such as making inferences, questions for a whole week might be focused on that skill. Students can record the number of correct responses they complete each day on a chart. If the number of responses remains the same week by week, students will have a running record of their achievement in reading comprehension.

Additional Note—Bell drills take a little more time to complete than Word of the Day and Daily Oral Language activities. For this reason, Bell Drills for reading comprehension might be completed twice a week. Bell drills can be selected with skill groups in mind. If reading selections are provided on half sheets of letter-sized paper, students can be provided with reading selections at their own levels. All class members can answer questions designed to reinforce the same targeted comprehension skill with reading selections written at their independent reading levels. Students with the same readings can be assigned to read their selections aloud to the whole group and answer the questions assigned to their reading. Other members of the class can practice the comprehension skill by listening to the reading selection and determining the accuracy of the other students' responses.

2. Games such as question-and-answer quiz show formats, Bingo, pantomime, blackboard baseball, concentration, and hit-the-target can be useful in maintaining high levels of student motivation and engagement.

Quiz show formats—Engage students in generating review questions. Individuals or small groups of students can be given blank 3"x 5" cards for recording questions. Answers to each question should be written on the back of each card. To avoid duplication of questions, assign each individual or group a different topic or section of a book from which to generate questions. After collecting the questions, check for accuracy and coverage of material targeted for review. Sort the cards into categories and assign a point value to each. Arrange the cards on a project board that has been constructed with rows of library pockets. To play the game, assign students to small groups. Allow each group to select the questions category and level of difficulty. If the group members answer correctly, the group earns the points for the questions. If the group does not answer correctly, the next group in the rotation is allowed to attempt to answer the question. If this game is being used to assist the group in reviewing for a test, it is beneficial to allow students to use notes and consult each other within their assigned groups. The group with the most points at the end of the game wins. An alternative method for determining the outcome of the game is to assign a targeted number of points that each group should attempt to earn. All groups that meet or exceed their target number of points are considered to be winners.

The project board can be constructed to look like the drawing on the following page.

The Quiz Show

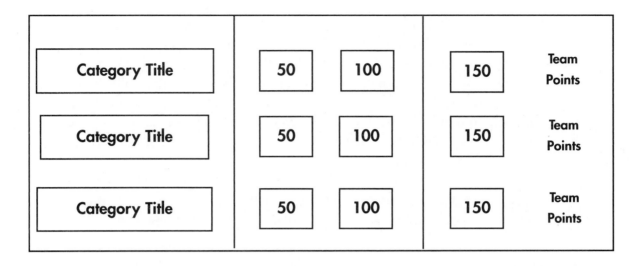

Academic Bingo—select targeted onsets and/or rhymes, vocabulary words, nonfiction elements, fiction elements, characters from stories read, or main ideas and supporting details from non-fiction reading selections. Provide each student with a blank Bingo grid (5 spaces across and 5 spaces down). Write targeted content on the board or provide each student with a copy of a completed grid. Instruct students to write or cut and paste the targeted content items in any order they chose on the blank Bingo grid. After the Bingo grids are completed, orally present clues. Students take turns identifying the correct answer to each clue. All students cover the targeted item each time a clue is identified if that item is on their card. Students win Bingo by completing a horizontal, vertical, or diagonal row, filling their whole card, or covering the items in each of the 4 corners. Agree upon the criteria for calling Bingo before announcing the clues.

Pantomime—Write vocabulary words on blank 3"x 5" index cards. Students take turns silently providing clues by acting out the meaning of the vocabulary word on their card.

Blackboard Baseball—Draw a baseball diamond on the board. Divide the class into two teams. Use questions written on 3" x 5" index cards. Provide students with time prior to the beginning of the game to study with a partner. Each person on the team takes a turn answering a question. Players advance around the bases as each person answers his or her question correctly. Magnets with students' names on them can be used to mark their position on the field. An incorrect answer is recorded as a strike. When a team accumulates three strikes, the team is out and the other team begins to answer questions. In this game, team members may not help   each other during their time at "bat."

Concentration—Write questions on one set of cards and answers on another set of cards. If students are learning to match sounds with letters, pictures can be used instead of words. Shuffle the cards and place them face down on a large, flat surface. Students take turns turning over two cards. If the cards match, the student keeps the pair. If the cards do not match, students turn the cards face down and leave the cards in their original places. The game ends when all cards have been matched. The person with the highest number of pairs wins. This game can be played by one to four students at a time.

Hit-the-Target—Prepare a large, plastic tablecloth with a 5 box by 5 box grid. Use water-based markers to write letters, words, or simple drawings in each box.

Use bean bags or sponge blocks for students to throw. When a bean bag or sponge lands on a square, ask the student a question about the letter, word, or drawing. Students earn a point for each correct answer. If letters are written in the boxes, ask students to name a word that begins or ends with the letter hit. If words are in the boxes, ask students to think of another word that rhymes with the word in the box, has the same onset or rhyme as the word in the box, or is a synonym or antonym of the word in the box. If drawings are placed in the boxes, ask students to identify the beginning letter, ending letter, vowel sound, or vocabulary word that corresponds to the drawing.

3. A percentage of students respond most effectively to tactile-kinesthetic materials. Review materials that actively engage students' minds and hands include response cards, flip chutes, and student-constructed electronic file folder games.

Response Cards (Heward, Gardner, Cavanaugh, Courson, Grossi, & Barbetta, 1996)—Select a targeted skill to review and questions to ask students that have a limited number of potential responses (yes or no/ two-to-four letters/two to four vocabulary words/punctuations marks). Provide students with blank index cards on which to record each response (one per card). Ask the class a question. Provide 5-7 seconds of wait time. Instruct students to raise the correct card on a signal. All students remain engaged and active.

Flip Chutes—Engage students in constructing a flip chute for use with flash cards. Students look at one side of the flashcard, say the answer, put the card in the flip chute, and check their accuracy when the card exits from the bottom of the flip chute.

Materials
- Empty, Clean, and Dry Half Gallon Orange Juice Container
- Masking Tape or Clear Packing Tape
- Tag Board or Used File Folder
- Scissors
- Exacto Knife
- Ruler
- Pen
- Contact Paper (Optional)

Instructions
1. Draw a line 1 1/2" from the bottom and 1 1/2" from the top crease (where the carton begins to fold into a triangle).

2. Draw a line 2" from the bottom and 2" from the crease at the top of the carton.

3. Cut a 1/2" slot at the top and the bottom of the carton that spans the width of the carton on the face marked.

4. Cut 2 strips from the tag board 3 1/2" x 6" and 3 1/2" x 8 1/2".

5. Fold the longer piece of tag board 1/2" from one end.

6. Tape the folded end on the bottom of the bottom slot on the outside of the carton.

7. Fold the shorter piece of tag board 1/2" on both ends.

8. Tape the folded edges on the outside of the top slot and the outside of the bottom slot.

9. Cut the top spout area as far as the creases.

10. Tape the top flaps flat.

11. Cover with contact paper.

Electronic File Folder Game—Students can construct electronic file folder games with used file folders, aluminum foil, brass brads, and masking tape. Games can be saved and reused from year to year.

Materials
- Folder
- Brass Brads
- Masking Tape
- Aluminum Foil
- Clear Plastic Paper Protector
- Continuity Tester
- Batteries
- Pen

Instructions
1. Cut the flap off the side of the folder.

2. Cut the front of the folder 1/2" from the folded edge to within 1/2" from the top of the folder.

3. Slide the plastic protector on the front of the folder.

4. Tape the folder together on the back to secure the plastic protector.

5. Mark places for brads at regular intervals.

6. Punch holes with a pen.

7. Put brads in place.

8. Cut foil into strips.

9. Fold the foil two or three times.

10. Connect the brads that will be used to designate correct answers with foil strips.

11. Place masking tape over the foil.

12. Tape the folder closed.

13. Record the correct answer pattern on the back of the folder.

4. Teaching students to assist each other in reviewing basic skills by establishing a class-wide peer tutoring program can be an effective and efficient use of instructional time. Each student can be given a re-sealable baggie and a set of blank flashcards upon which to paste pictures or write letters, words, definitions, or phrases. At regularly scheduled times, peer buddies can drill each other on individual target skills or listen to each other re-read targeted selections in order to build fluency. All students benefit from (a) regular opportunities to review, (b) learning to provide and corrective positive feedback as a tutor, and (c) learning to accept positive and corrective feedback as a tutee. Before student pairs begin to work together, it is important to teach students to follow specific rules and procedures during the peer buddy tutoring sessions. Students need direct instruction and opportunities to role play the feedback processes established for the class.

SPELLING

Phonics games are easily adapted to whole-group activities. Board games can be played with each student having his or her own set of cards. Quiz show type games and traditional spelling bees can also be used to pull the group together despite varying levels of ability. The teacher simply calls out questions and words related to each student's ability level as the game progresses. Independent practice can follow, using the same set of words or phonics skills practiced during the game.

Board games can be developed around themes, holidays, and seasons. These are easy to file. Copies can be given to students for use at home. Floor mats made of poster board or cheap fabric can be used with bean bags. Letters can be printed on the mats. Students generate words that include letters the bean bags land on. Cubes made of milk cartons covered with paper, or wooden blocks can also be used. The cubes might have vowels on one side and consonants on the other. As students roll the cubes, they must think of words that contain the vowels and consonants that come up.

LANGUAGE

Language activities can be an enjoyable time for the class when activities such as the following are presented.

1. Sing traditional or modern songs from printed sheets. Students can identify parts of speech by circling nouns with blue, verbs with red, and adjectives with yellow.

2. Make a wall chart of all the capitalization and punctuation rules appropriate to the grade levels represented by the class. Each day provide the class with two-to-four incorrectly written sentences on the chalkboard. The students can use the rules on the chart to correct the sentences orally as the teacher marks their corrections on the chalkboard. This activity only takes 5-to-10 minutes. It is an excellent way to focus the group's attention while practicing skills on many levels simultaneously.

3. Make "word walls" with seasonal or academic themes. Categorization, parts of speech, sentences, paragraphs, dictionary skills, and vocabulary development lessons can be developed

from student-generated word lists.

4. Tape record plays complete with sound effects. Because less movement and direct interaction are needed, taped plays can be an excellent first step in learning group participation without overwhelming the students. The tape can then be played over the school intercom or be placed in a listening center for recreational reinforcement time.

5. Use pantomime to sharpen vocabulary skills. Pantomiming words can generate ideas for synonyms, antonyms, and multiple meanings for words.

6. Use newspaper comic strips cut apart to sharpen sequencing and prediction skills.

7. Use comic strips with words covered up to encourage story writing.

8. Make group-produced books. Use stories, poems, and illustrations from each class member.

GENERAL GUIDELINES

In short, when planning instruction for a multilevel group, gear oral instruction to the overall chronological age level. Keep independent practice work at the academic functioning level of each individual. Continually work toward bringing the two levels together.

In the beginning and at times of increased stress, keep in mind that the success of the group hinges on keeping all aspects of instruction in perspective. If behavior management takes extra time, be flexible. Taking extra time when the class needs it actually saves time in the long run. As important as teaching math, reading, and writing is, it is never more important than helping students deal with their behavior. On the other hand, making real progress academically reinforces positive self-concepts. Students often think that they are stupid and incapable of learning because of their failure to master material others have mastered. They need to make progress academically. They also need to take the time necessary to learn appropriate behavior. Help them keep the two needs balanced. Students won't feel successful unless they can see progress in both areas.

Maintaining instructional focus helps de-escalate the most disruptive behaviors. As Marcus and Lydel illustrate, not all problems can be totally avoided.

ANECDOTE

"Yo mamma!"

"Don't you talk 'bout my mamma! I'm gonna kill you, Sucker!"

"Mrs. R., Lydel is hitting me."

"Lydel. Marcus. Come here. Sit in your chairs. Tell me what is happening." As if I don't know.

Fighting is a daily ritual. "Yo mamma" doesn't mean anything to anyone. It's just a phrase repeated at predetermined intervals to signal the ceremonial rite of sparring. Any rational attempt to problem-solve is met with shrugs of disbelief. As far as the children are concerned, only a novice would perceive the bashing in of heads as a problem to be solved diplomatically. And yet, here I sit day after day repeating my words and hearing theirs again.

"Marcus was messing with me."

"No, I wasn't! Lydel was talking 'bout my mamma. No one talks 'bout my mamma!"

"You liar!"

"OK boys. First of all, what is the rule about fighting?"

Lydel speaks first with, "Keep your hands and feet to yourself. Go to the teacher if you need help."

Marcus retorts, "But Lydel was messing with me. My mamma says if anyone messes with me I 'posed to fight."

"Marcus, at home you do what your mother tells you to do. At school, the rules are different. Fighting at school is inappropriate."

"My mamma says fight, so I'm gonna fight!"

"If you decide to fight at school, what will happen?"

"I don't care what you say, bitch! You aren't my mamma! You aren't nothing to me!"

"I'm asking a question. What will happen if you and Lydel decide to fight?"

Marcus sulks and lifts his middle finger in my direction. Lydel giggles as he shifts his weight back and forth in his chair.

"OK guys, I need an answer. Either we can discuss this and come up with an agreement together or you can each write your own plans. Either way, neither of you will be earning work sign-offs or points until it is done."

"Fuck you!"

"We need to talk appropriately, Marcus. I'll know you are ready when you raise your hand."

Lydel hesitantly raises his hand. "Yes, Lydel."

"If I fight at school, I will get in trouble." "Why?"

"Because fighting's not right." "Why?"

"Because someone might get hurt."

"That's right Lydel. Thank you. I see Marcus has his hand raised. Are you ready to talk with us?"

"Yeah."

"Are there other things people can do when they are mad?" "Yeah."

"What?"

"Ignore or ask for help."

"Anything else?"

"Don't say or do things to make other people mad."

"OK, Lydel, anything else?"

"Just walk away."

"How does your body feel when you get mad? Are your muscles tight or relaxed?"

"Tight!"

"Do you have lots of energy, or are you kind of sleepy?"

"I feel like punching!"

"Marcus, how do you feel when you're mad?"

"I just feel mad like I could knock you out!"

"Well, that energy is hard to deal with sometimes. Ignoring someone who is doing or saying something aggravating doesn't get rid of that energy, does it?"

"No way!"

"What can we do with that energy?"

"Scream!"

"Run!"

"Punch pillows!"

"Jump up and down!"

"Stomp!"

"Scribble!"

"OK, now you're thinking! Once again, the problem is what?"

"Fighting!"

"The feeling is what?"

"Anger!"

"The appropriate choices are.. "

"Ignore."

"Ask for help."

"Walk away."

"Don't say or do inappropriate things."

"What can you do with the extra energy?"

"Ask if it is OK to do something appropriate that takes extra energy."

"If you decide to fight, what will you earn?"

"Time in the corner."

"No activity period."

"No points or money for the classroom store."

"No friends."

"If you follow your plan, what will you earn?"

"Points and money for the store."

"Activity time."

"Treats."

"More friends."

"Which would you rather earn?"

In unison the boys say, "The good stuff!"

"So, what are you going to do?"

"Talk nicely."

"Stop fighting."

"I like your plans. You will get a chance to show me your new decisions in action tomorrow. For the rest of today, however, you will do your work in in-class suspension. You can earn work sign-offs and money for correctly completed work, but you will not earn points or recess privileges until tomorrow.

6

Dealing with Changes

The class is moving along very nicely. The teacher, aide, and students have all found a balance. A sense of trust and stability is beginning to form. Then something happens. A student moves away. A new student arrives. A substitute is called. Art is moved from Monday to Wednesday this week. A holiday provides a break in the usual routine. Whatever the change is, the class will respond. It is not the teacher's fault. Changes—even pleasant changes—can over-stimulate, threaten, and disrupt these children.

Do not be surprised, hurt, angered, or discouraged by the reactions of these students to changes in their routines. There are ways to get through and reduce the stress they feel. Dealing with changes and stress is a constructive part of their learning experience, so help them prepare and then help them cope.

NEW ADDITIONS TO THE CLASS

The addition of a new student to the class usually results in mixed reactions. Some students enjoy getting to know a new classmate. Other students resent the time and attention a new student requires or worry that people who had previously been their friends will stop liking them. The teacher cannot eliminate all of the stress and anxiety associated with the addition of a new student in the class. Much can be done, however, to reduce tension and facilitate the group's return to a more typical routine.

1. Give the class 2 or 3 days notice if a classmate is leaving or a new student is arriving. Some of the anxiety over the changes can be handled prior to the arrival of the new student through discussion and role playing.
2. Ask the students how they felt when they were new to the class. Discuss ways to help the new student feel welcome.
3. Engage the students in preparing the new student's desk, bulletin board space, and instructional materials.
4. Construct a student-generated card or banner to welcome the new classmate.
5. Prepare a snack, special game, or song to welcome the new classmate.
6. Give students a role in introducing the new classmate to the classroom routine, cafeteria, special outside classes such as art or music, and media center.

7. Be prepared to give consideration to students' requests for reassurance that they are still valued even after the new classmate arrives.

SCHEDULE CHANGES

Each morning, review the day's schedule. Use pictures or graphics along with words to help students who may not be as proficient at reading. Whether there are changes or not, discuss events of the day in order. On days when changes may take place, this discussion and preparation time will already be an established part of the routine. Letting students know at 8:00 that PE will be at 10:00 instead of 1:00 gives them time to adjust to the idea.

Keep holiday celebrations simple and well structured. Free time can be a disaster for students with poor academic and behavior management skills. After an extended holiday, the class may need a reorientation period much like the beginning of school. Review rules. Role play. Write and illustrate stories about the application of the rules and expectations. And, remember that regression is common, but it can be minimized by providing extra structure until the class recovers its sense of balance and trust. The following are the most important things to remember during times of change:

a. The children will act out their anxiety.
b. It is not the teacher's fault.
c. Their anxiety will subside with reassurance and a return to structure.
d. Planning ahead for, as well as problem solving after, a change—with the students' participation—can reduce disruption and helps to teach students to handle stress.
e. Changes are an opportunity for growth despite the chaotic outward appearance.
f. During times of stress:
   1. Decrease academic pressure by providing practice sheets of previously mastered material.
   2. Increase structure by limiting interactions among students and keeping them actively involved with tasks.
   3. Increase the frequency of rewards.
   4. Use primary reinforcers such as food and drink.

SUBSTITUTES

Give the students a plan for dealing with substitutes. Let them know what rewards are available for those who behave appropriately. Let them know that a substitute won't do everything just like the teacher. Point out that the substitute is in charge. Share the substitute day folder with the class. The folder should contain a seating chart (with photographs of students if at all possible), work assignments, point sheet and behavior management instructions, a daily schedule, and any information that is essential about each student, such as medication or behavior patterns.

Including the Behavior Bingo cards in the substitute folder is a great way to encourage the substitute to review the class rules positively at the beginning of the day. Students will feel reassured that the adult knows the rules and will respond more appropriately to the temporary change in routine.

PROFANITY

Profanity and name calling are common events during times of change and increased stress. Whether to ignore this behavior or provide consequences for it depends on the reasons for the inappropriate talk.

With very young children who may be using profanity to shock and gain extra attention, ignoring them until they talk appropriately often works best.

For older children, an adult who ignores profanity might be perceived as weak. Their respect and trust might be weakened if they feel that the adult is either unable or unwilling to stand up to them. Older children and adolescents feel that a personal attack requires some kind of action. It will be difficult for them to accept alternative methods of handling problems if the adult in charge is seen as weak.

Care must be taken to keep inappropriate interactions in perspective. A child may use profanity as a smoke screen to avoid consequences for other behavior. Make sure to give consequences for both the inappropriate behavior and language.

The following anecdote demonstrates how to deal with both inappropriate language and actions.

ANECDOTE

Jason throws a balled-up piece of paper across the room.

"Jason, please pick up the paper."

"Shut up, whore!"

"If you need help with your work, I will help you. But, first you need to pick up your paper and do 5 minutes for inappropriate language."

"Fucker!"

"That's 10 minutes. You have to the count of three to pick up your paper, or I'll help you. One.., two"

"Oh, all right, you four-eyed, flat-chested, big-hipped heifer! Don't get your panties in a wad! I'm going!" Jason stomps across the room, snatches the paper, and marches to the cool-off carrel.

He earns a "0" in appropriate interactions and on-task behavior, but he has followed directions and is getting more creative with expressing anger. Once we've conquered "curse" words, we'll concentrate on finding ways for him to express anger that won't get him into trouble. One step at a time.

Even in the midst of a problem, the teacher should look and listen for small signs of growth. When a child is calm, share it with him.

"Jason, your 10 minutes are up. Please come to your seat." Jason slumps in his chair. "I can't do this junk."

"You've only been here 3 days. I don't expect you to know it all yet. But before we work on the spelling, I want to tell you something I noticed just now."

"What?"

"The first morning you were here, you must have used about 200 curse words. Just now you stopped after using only two."

"Yeah. I did, didn't I? I'm sorry I called you those names. I was mad."

"1 know. Thank you for apologizing. But for now, think about the self-control you decided to use. You used only two curse words; you picked up the paper on your own even though you were mad; and you did your 10 minutes in cool-off. Now you have all but two of your points, and there is still time to complete this work for a work sign-off and money for the classroom store."

"I'm not always bad."

"No. You're not. You are capable of making decisions that will help you instead of hurt you. You've already proven that many times in the past few days, and that's not bad at all! Now, are you ready to get this spelling done?"

"OK." Jason smiles and sits up straighter in his chair as we begin to work on his spelling together.

"Jason."

"Yeah."

"One more thing before I go to help Tommy..."

"What?"

"The next time your work is hard to understand, just raise your hand. Ms. Agnew and I love to help kids with their work. If you didn't need our help, we'd be out of our jobs, and that would be terrible!"

"OK."

"Thanks!"

Jason is all smiles as I walk toward Tommy's desk. They're being easy on me today. They're having their problems one at a time.

7

Parent/Teacher Relations

In spite of increasing evidence that emotional and behavioral disturbances are caused by biological disorders, parents are still the first to be blamed for a child's problems (Koplewicz, 1996). When a child has mental retardation, a heart condition, cerebral palsy, asthma, or diabetes, educators tend to react with compassion toward the child and the parents. Collaboration among parents, teachers, and other professionals proceeds as outlined in local, state, and federal laws governing services for students with special needs. When a student has an emotional and behavioral disorder, however, the parents may feel embarrassed. Some parents fear that they will be treated with disrespect and that their child will be stigmatized. These parents often attempt to hide the child's treatment history. In one middle school where I worked as a Varying Exceptionalities Specialist, a young man was brought to me for disciplinary reasons. He had never been identified as having a disability in spite of a long history of truancy, noncompliance with routine requests, and poor grades. When I asked why he was not being evaluated for special education services, teachers and administrators told me that he was just a nasty kid—that nothing was wrong with him. As he sat in my office, he began to draw pictures. I asked him about the pictures. As we talked, he began to reveal a very disturbing history of suicide attempts, hospitalizations, anxiety, and depression. He and his mother both suffered from bi-polar disorder. His father was in prison for attempting to murder him and his mother. When I presented this information to school personnel, they refused to believe that it was true. With his mother's consent, I obtained a copy of his hospital records that confirmed the stories that he and his mother had shared with me. The nasty, noncompliant, underachieving, discipline problem brought to my office that day was a young man in severe distress. I asked his mother why she had never alerted the school. She said that she was afraid to tell anyone. She had asked for help 3 or 4 years before our conversation and had been told that she just needed to quit babying her son and making excuses for him.

Those of us who choose to work with students who have challenging academic and behavioral problems need to educate our peers, other parents, and the students themselves about the nature of their disabilities. It is not their fault that they have medical conditions—differences in the ways that their brains and bodies produce and metabolize a variety of chemicals (neurotransmitters) that regulate attention, reality processing, and mood. While chaotic home environments, exposure to trauma, and inconsistent behavior management at home and in the school can certainly have a detrimental effect on students' behaviors and emotional health, parents should not be blamed for their child's biological predisposition to behavior and emotional disorders.

Some parents and guardians are so overwhelmed by their own situations that they are unable to assist the teacher with academic and behavioral problems. Other parents feel as confused, angry, and defeated as their children. These parents may lash out at the teacher, blaming the school for the child's problems. They may give in to the child out of despair. Some may be caught up in a cycle of abuse, neglect, and overindulgence as they struggle with their own feelings about a child who is exhausting to handle. And some parents are doing a wonderful job, but need occasional reassurance and guidance.

O'Shea, O'Shea, Algozzine, and Hammitte (2001) describe five stages of grief and acceptance that parents often experience when dealing with a child who has a disability. Denial is often the first reaction to information that a child's development is not typical. Parents will discount the seriousness of a behavior or emotional reaction by making statements such as "He's just being a boy." or "All kids get a little wound up once in a while." If teachers, mental health professionals, or pediatricians suggest a disorder that the parents don't believe is appropriate for their child, they will often go to another professional, friend, or family member for a different diagnosis. This is a tough time for the professionals who are trying to help, because parents usually refuse to give permission for assessments as well as treatment. Educators can be helpful during this time by continuing to offer information, respecting the parents' rights, discussing the benefits of particular options, and encouraging the parents to view school personnel as advocates for them and their child. Demanding that a parent make a decision, criticizing the parent, or expressing frustration over the child's behavior will often result in causing the parent to be less open to assistance.

The second stage of grief and acceptance is often characterized by anger and guilt. Parents, particularly mothers, wonder if they ate something or participated in some activity during the prenatal period that caused the disability. If the child is older before a problem is recognized, the parents may blame each other, other family members, doctors, teachers, or neighbors. Educators sometimes feel like they are damned if they do and damned if they don't when a parent is experiencing this stage of generalized anger and guilt. It is tempting to respond to angry parents with indignation. We might think, "How dare you attack me? I'm the one person in this world who happens to care about your rudely behaved child!" The most effective strategy for assisting a parent who is angry and blaming, however, is to listen; praise the parent for caring; empathize with the parent's frustrations and fears; and continue to emphasize a team approach—making it clear that you are joining with the parent to be an advocate for the child. Underneath the anger and guilt is the overwhelming thought that the child might not ever overcome the present challenges and lead a productive life. Parents may reject the ones most prepared to be of assistance, but it is the teacher's job to keep the door open for potential intervention, information, and hope.

As parents stop blaming themselves and others, they may begin to attempt to make bargains. These bargains sometimes take the form of prayers—asking God to spare the child in exchange for some penance the parent is prepared to pay. They may also investigate every possible treatment option, believing that if they do everything perfectly, they will be able to cure the child. Educators are often pressured to implement the latest fad, scam, or folk remedy. It is important for educators to listen, help the parent separate fact from hype, and remain committed to the shared best interest of the child.

Once parents realize that the child is not going to be cured, depression may overwhelm them. They may accept help from anyone who is willing to do the work themselves, but refuse to invest time and energy into implementing strategies at home and in the community. Sometimes parents stop interacting with family members and friends. During this time, educators can get the impression that a parent just doesn't care. That is a dangerous assumption—one that can lead to a total breakdown in services for a young person as the experience with the middle school student described earlier in this chapter illustrates. If a parent is unresponsive, it is especially important to make the effort to communicate regularly. Send notes through the mail, email the parent if an email address is available, leave voicemail messages, and send messages through mutual acquaintances. Routine progress reports and annual educational planning meetings are not sufficient. This parent needs to believe that there is a reason to keep trying—that even if the young person will not be cured, he or she still has opportunities to learn, grow, improve, and work toward a better quality of life. Having a consistently positive person in the life of both the parents and the child during periods when the parents are tempted to quit trying is essential to the child's future and the parents' movement toward acceptance.

With acceptance parents are ready to become active in the treatment of their own child's challenges and to reach out to other parents. Parents who have reached the stage of acceptance often give of their time to mentor parents at earlier stages, provide respite care, lead support groups, and work to change policies and laws at the local, state, and federal levels. The Council for Exceptional Children (CEC), the Council for Children with Behavioral Disorders (CCBD), the National Alliance for People with Mental Illness (NAMI), and the Federation of Families are among the national and international organizations with which parents can become involved.

The following anecdote is shared as an illustration of one mother's movement through the stages of grief and acceptance. One mother of a young man I have known over a 15 year period came to me when he was about 5 years old. Gordon was an impish blue-eyed redhead with many freckles on his face. He could be quite charming one-on-one when he and his mother stopped for brief visits. He had an outstanding vocabulary and was interested in a wide variety of topics. Longer visits that included more people were disastrous. He would race in and out of rooms, slam doors, yell, grab items out of people's hands without warning, and spit on anyone who annoyed him. His mother would attempt to stop him to no avail. Play dates with other children in the neighborhood ended early with some, if not all, of the children in attendance crying. Gordon appeared to be the happiest when he had created the most chaos. Mom argued with anyone who even suggested that Gordon needed help. She thought that everyone just picked on him. The pediatrician had diagnosed Gordon with attention deficit hyperactivity disorder (ADHD) when he was 2 years old. Mom did not believe the pediatrician. Gordon was dismissed from four preschool programs. Mom said that the people who ran those programs were idiots and didn't know what they were doing. After the public school called Mom for a conference about Gordon's behavior, she called me. She was furious! A psychologist had evaluated Gordon with Mom's permission and determined that Gordon had ADHD and oppositional defiant disorder (ODD). The pediatrician and psychologist had both suggested that Gordon be evaluated by a psychiatrist for medication. Mom was opposed to medication and did not know what to do. She trusted me, so we talked. I told Mom about the risks to Gordon educationally and emotionally if he continued to have such a hard time controlling his behavior. She stated that she could handle him and was worried that he would abuse drugs when he was a teenager if she gave him drugs now. I empathized with her situation. Wanting only what is best for your child and having so little proof that what the professionals tell you is the right thing to do is a scary situation. She asked what I thought. I told her that (a) she had to do what she thought was best for Gordon; (b) that I believed that if she decided to put him on medication she would carefully monitor his progress, and stop the medication if it was not the right decision; and (c) that Gordon would be more at risk for drug and alcohol abuse, school failure, and juvenile justice involvement in the future if he was not able to focus on academics and follow teachers' directions now. Then I asked her how Gordon felt about it. She began to cry. She said that Gordon begged her every night to do something. She told me how he cried himself to sleep saying, "I don't want to be a bad boy." When she stopped crying, I told her that I thought she knew what she needed to do. She agreed. She could not bear to watch Gordon suffer any longer.

A few months later Gordon and Mom came to visit. Gordon stopped in the living room long enough to tell me about school, his new friends, and the happy face note his teacher had given him to bring home before he ran out to the backyard to play with my children. Mom reported that Gordon was responding quite well to the medication and the behavior management system that she, the school, and the psychologist had developed together. Gordon spent 2 years in a resource program for students with emotional and behavioral problems before being dismissed into fulltime general education classes. Gordon is in his 20s now. He attends college and is doing well. He is fortunate that his mother moved quickly through the stages of denial, anger, bargaining, depression, and acceptance. Gordon's school and life experiences could have been much different if he had not had such a responsive parent and school environment.

While the teacher cannot be a psychologist, social worker, police officer, and recreational director while fulfilling the role of educator, he or she can be a valuable resource to parents who are able and willing to benefit from information made available to them.

The following anecdotes are from real experiences with parents.

FALSE ACCUSATIONS OF TEACHER MISCONDUCT

Parents at times have falsely accused teachers of prejudice, neglect, unprovoked hostility, unfair consequences, and other offenses. Some parents are overprotective and overemotional when it comes to their child. A teacher must take care to be precise with the parent as well as the student about both rewards and punishments. Frequent communication helps. When the student is clearly attempting to set up a triangle of opposition, it is important to get the parent, student, teacher, and at least one other staff member together in a face-to-face conference in which facts are presented. Even faced with facts, the parent may continue to deny that the child is being less than truthful. Threats of refusal of services, going to the school board, and even lawsuits may follow. Continue to stick to the facts; keep clear, concise records; keep supervisors notified of threats; and treat the child with caring, consistent discipline. The child is not responsible for the parent's behavior. Try to keep that in mind even though the child is contributing to the problems by exaggerating or telling lies. Remember that all children stretch the truth from time to time. It is the parent, not the child, who decides what to do with the information. Having the child write a sentence or two about what is going on at the end of each period can sometimes help reorient and reduce the wild stories taken home.

At the meeting, the parent will often be embarrassed for believing the child. It may come out that this has happened before. Reassure the parent. Let him or her know that it is right to care about the child's welfare. Compliment the parent's willingness to get involved. Then work out a plan for communicating in the future. It is good for the child to be present during this discussion, so that he or she knows that the adults are communicating with each other; that there is a plan for avoiding future difficulties; and that nothing is being plotted behind the child's back. This will not completely stop the manipulative behavior of the child, and the parent may need time to come to trust the teacher. However, this procedure will slow the problem down to a manageable speed.

LACK OF PARENT INVOLVEMENT

The parent who never shows up for a meeting, can't be reached by phone, and returns few if any written notes has clearly given up. It might be too late, but just in case it isn't, be persistent. Continue to make phone calls. Write notes for the child to take home. Send a weekly or monthly postcard through the mail. Be positive! This parent can't take any more bad news about the child's behavior. Find something good to say. Write, "Joe has a beautiful smile. It really brightens my day." You don't have to add that he only smiled once in a week full of cursing, vandalizing, and fighting. Or, "Mark's handwriting is really improving." Don't include the fact that you haven't finished counting the number of items he has defaced with profane language while practicing his handwriting.

If the parent never shows signs of taking an interest, it is sad for the child. This is even more reason for the teacher to provide a nurturing as well as disciplined classroom. The child can benefit from the care and teaching he or she receives at school. Helping the child learn to function in society as a whole no matter what the rules at home might be is a must.

BRIDGING THE GAP

Some parents have conquered a great deal in their own lives and have a deep understanding of their child's needs. These parents are doing well. They know how to care for their child in helpful ways. But they are tired and sometimes discouraged. Living with a child who has an emotional or behavioral disorder is exhausting. These parents need encouragement and occasional support in the form of information about behavior management, child care opportunities, and other community support services. It is generally extremely satisfying to work with such parents.

One of the most valuable things teachers can do for these parents is to help them learn to apply behavior management techniques at home. Give the parents a few basic rules to follow, then help them brainstorm ideas based on the rules. The rules I give parents are as follows:

1. Select no more than two behaviors to work on at a time.

2. Select observable, enforceable behaviors to correct. For example, "Put all personal belongings in their correct places when not in use," instead of, "Be neater."

3. Have a hierarchy of rewards and punishments. Use rewards when at all possible.

4. Make sure rewards and punishments relate to the behavior. Having a child scrub the entire driveway for pouring tempera paint down one side of it makes more sense than sending the child to bed early. Likewise, a reward in the form of one new color of paint per week for appropriate use of the paint makes more sense than giving the child a candy bar.

5. Do not demand immediate mastery. If the child has been screaming for 5 hours per day, start out by rewarding the child for reducing this to 4 or less hours of screaming per day.

6. Have a plan to follow. The child will probably increase the inappropriate behavior in the beginning just to see whether the parents are really serious. Stick to the plan for at least 2 to 3 weeks.

7. The plan will work best if all members of the family participate in helping the child learn the new behavior.

8. Base all rewards and punishments on known likes and dislikes of the child.

9. Be as matter-of-fact about the plan as possible when sharing it with the child.

BRIBERY VS. BEHAVIOR MANAGEMENT

Occasionally parents will object to behavior modification techniques used in the classroom because they see them as a form of bribery. Explaining the difference between behavior management and bribery requires a clear understanding of the steps involved in both. When a child is in the midst of a tantrum and an adult says "Act right, and I will give you a cookie," that is bribery. Children learn that trick early. Every time someone tells them "No," they go into action.

With behavior modification, the emphasis is on prevention of inappropriate behavior through the initial rewarding of appropriate choices the student makes. The student is told before a problem arises what rewards and punishments are available to him. He is then told that he may decide which ones he wants to earn. This is no more a form of bribery than signing a contract to receive payment for a job when the job is completed satisfactorily. Relating the behavior management system to the work world makes it easier for parents to understand and accept.

THE INITIAL PARENT/TEACHER MEETING

The initial meeting between the parent and the teacher can and should set a productive tone. The teacher should come to the meeting with an outline of the behavior management plan used in the classroom, a sample point sheet, and a written list of materials the child will need to bring to school. Don't be surprised if, a week or two later, the parent requests another conference to review the point sheet and behavior management plan. These can be overwhelming to the parent in the beginning. Make sure to discuss any policies the school has about restraining students. Get written permission for this if it is allowed and may be needed. Also ask about any allergies. Some parents object to their children eating items cooked in class. If the class cooks regularly, discuss this with the parent.

Let the parent take the lead in how much is covered in the first meeting. Some parents have a lot of useful information to share with the teacher, while others are hesitant. Being prepared, positive, and professional is the best approach to take.

EXAMPLES OF PARENT/TEACHER COMMUNICATIONS

1. Phone conferences. Call parents at least twice a semester to report positive behavior and academic progress.

2. Daily point sheets. Write brief notes on them as often as necessary. Be positive.

3. Weekly or biweekly "good behavior" notes. These can be preprinted with fill-in-the-blank type messages. Put them in work folders or staple them to the point sheet.

4. Weekly or biweekly work envelopes. Put samples of the student's work in the envelope. Have the parent sign the front of the envelope. The student can return and reuse the envelope.

5. Semester outlines for academic subjects.

6. Special event notices.

7. Face-to-face conferences.

8. Report cards.

9. Annual individualized education programs (IEPs).

It may not be necessary to do all of these things for all of the parents all of the time. These are merely suggestions that may help parents and teachers work more efficiently together.

GENERAL GUIDELINES

1. Keep parents informed.

2. Be as positive as possible as often as possible.

3. Discuss appropriate choices students have made when at all possible, even when problems arise that need to be shared with parents.

4. Keep a community resource file with names, phone numbers, and addresses of agencies that may offer assistance to families in any way.

5. Keep complete and accurate records. Share these records with the parents.

6. Provide parents with the names of books and articles that might help them manage the child more easily at home.

7. If problems arise between the parent and teacher, notify a supervisor immediately. Have another staff member present at all conferences. Keep copies of any letters and notes sent home.

8. The severity of the disability affects the initiation and progress of the stages of grief and acceptance.

9. As the child reaches important developmental milestones, parents may go through the stages of grief and acceptance again.

10. As the family reaches important transition periods, parents may go through the stages of grief and acceptance again.

11 The stages of grief and acceptance tend to be more cyclical than linear.

Dealing with the students for 5 to 6 hours per day, taking care of the seemingly endless paperwork, and then finding time to assist parents can get tiring. Chapter 8 discusses issues related to teacher burnout and how to prevent it.

8

Personal Notes

From behind the gimmicks and techniques involved in the survival of a day, week, year, or longer with children with behavioral disorders, a real person emerges. The children learn to trust the professional aspects of a teacher's relationship with them. However, children are never content to stop there, as adults might be. Children watch, wait, listen, pry, probe, and poke until they're satisfied that they know all that they want and need to know. The personality they discover behind the point sheets, reward system, and time-out chair makes all the difference as far as they're concerned.

My enthusiasm for teaching and learning is real. My belief in the children is real. My desire to be honest, fair, firm, and caring is real. In these ways, I believe most teachers are alike. I have a visual image of myself as a velvet-padded brick. The children's willful, misdirected energy can safely find release and new direction as they figuratively and sometimes literally bang their heads against me. I am not unforgivingly angered, disappointed, or hurt. No matter how rough the previous day was, I can meet a new day with positive expectations. My students know that I hate fights and angry confrontations. They also know I won't back down or be intimidated.

Not everyone is a velvet-padded brick. Not everyone needs to be. A teacher's style emerges from a creative blending of learned technique and individual personality. It is important for each teacher to be aware of his or her own personal style. In spite of all we know about behavior management, the real growth occurs through relationships.

As I watch my students go through the ups and downs of learning newer, more appropriate responses to their feelings, I am often amazed at little things adults can easily take for granted. Why does a child who has been interrupting a lesson for 10 solid minutes, ignoring corrections, and cursing a blue streak over the zeros on his point sheet respond quickly, quietly, and without further discussion to "Put your head on your desk—now"?

Then there is the 6-foot tall, 15-year-old who could break me into kindling if he wanted to. Why does he go to the chair in the corner when I tell him to go after he has just called me a four-eyed, fucking whore?

I'm not complaining, but sometimes the craziest things students do are the most compliant. It is part of a mystery I'm still trying to solve. The following tips are designed to maximize personal effectiveness and minimize stress. Burnout *can* be avoided.

1. Know your style, your strengths, and your limits.

2. Use your style and strengths at every possible point.

3. Respect your limits just as carefully as you respect the limits of your students. Asking for help when you need it is not just OK; it's the only sane, intelligent, and professional thing to do.

4. On rotten days, it's OK to tell the students that you feel angry, disappointed, or tired. Sometimes I am able to get through a tough day by saying, I really hate it when our day goes like this. I feel like having a screaming fit too." The students will smile devilishly and hope with all their might that I lose it. I then find it helpful to talk myself through the decision-making steps out loud. This helps diffuse my anger while setting an appropriate example for the children.

5. At some point, there will be a child who really annoys you or is repulsive to you in some way. Admit it to yourself. Discuss it confidentially with a co-worker. Be aware of it as you deal with the student. Being honest with yourself is the only way to get beyond it. Not liking every child is not a sign of failure. Making a conscious effort to be positive with the child in spite of your feelings can work. It's OK to have personal feelings. It's important to maintain professional behavior.

6. Have at least two fun activities always available for spur-of-the-moment rewards. Bingo for small prizes, craft activities, and simple cooking activities are common favorites.

7. Plan at least one thing every day that you enjoy doing with the class. I personally hate reading-group activities. Science experiments, singing with the guitar, and building structures related to social studies are my favorite activities. I can motivate myself and my students to get through less enjoyable lessons by planning something more fun for later.

8. Have highly structured, independent work always available for times when things get wild. Word searches, crossword puzzles, and fill-in-the-blank worksheets are possibilities. One thing that works well with older students is to offer them the choice of covering material orally in an appropriate way or having them copy a large amount of information from the chalkboard or a book. The message to them is, "We are going to cover this information today. You may benefit from a

discussion of it or, you may copy it. Either way, I will know you have been introduced to the concepts. You decide with your behavior how you will learn it."

9. Take weekends and holidays off. The paper work will be there waiting for you when you get back. Mental health breaks must be respected.

10. Have as much love and support in your life as possible. You can't give if you're not getting.

11. Make a list of all the things that need to be done. Organize them by day, week, grading period, and semester. Give the aide or associate the jobs that don't absolutely have to be done by the teacher. Filing, grading papers, recording grades, averaging grades, filling out forms, running off papers, and caring for bulletin boards are just a few of the time-consuming clerical chores that can be shared with others.

12. Give the aide or associate a list of expected responsibilities and do's and don'ts in the beginning. Appendix D gives some excerpts from my own files. Getting off to a good start by being positive and precise with the aide has many advantages. Be aware of how much training and experience the aide has. Some school systems employ well-educated associates, some do their own training, and others require very little education and training.

13. Set up a filing system immediately. It is easy to get lost in all the paper shuffling. School systems are funded to an extent based on the accuracy of their paperwork. Folder headings can fall under two main categories: Professional and Instructional.

Exhibit 8-1. Organizing Paperwork

PROFESSIONAL FOLDERS

These can be organized in the following way:

- Professional Documents:
    - ❑ Certificates
    - ❑ Diplomas
    - ❑ Evaluations
    - ❑ Awards and/or Grants
- Special Education Memos
- Regular Education Memos
- Testing Forms and Information
- Report Cards
- Anecdotal Records

- Behavior Charts and Graphs
- Motivational Charts and Graphs
- Lesson Plans
- Substitute Folder
- Associate Folder
- Classroom Management File
- Forms:
    - ❏ Blank IEP Forms
    - ❏ Blank Conference Forms
    - ❏ Blank Re-evaluation Forms
    - ❏ Informed Consent Documents
- Permission Slips
- Acronym Lists for County, State, and Federal Programs
- Community Resource List for Parents

INSTRUCTIONAL FOLDERS

Have a folder for each month of the year. Attach a blank calendar to the front of each folder with the name of the month printed on it. Make notes on the calendar for quick reference to special holidays and activity sheets you may find related to each month. Stick copies of all monthly activities in these folders. Art, math, spelling, science, and social studies can be included in these special activity folders. Building a reservoir of "filler" activities can save your life on hectic days. These activities are often useful to have in the substitute folder. The substitute can keep students busy on current activities without disrupting plans you have made. Make sure the substitute folder is updated each month. Christmas worksheets won't go over well in May. Label these special monthly activity folders.

- Addition Worksheets
- Subtraction Worksheets
- Multiplication Worksheets
- Division Worksheets
- Spelling
- Language
- Primary Reading
- Upper Elementary Reading
- Secondary Reading
- Teacher-Selected Science Topics
- Teacher-Selected Social Study Topics

14. Plan bulletin boards with seasons in mind. The background paper takes a long time to replace and is expensive. September through November background paper can be brown, yellow, or orange. December through February background can be red, dark blue, or white. March through June background can be pink, light green, or light blue. During the summer months, primary colors work well. Each month,

borders and actual decorations can be changed in a minimum of time. Change background paper a minimum of every 3 months.

15 Make large monthly or seasonal envelopes out of poster board. Print headings on each, and file bulletin board materials in them. Use a large, heavy-duty garbage bag or sew a cloth bag to hold all the envelopes for easy storage.

16. Keep an "Idea Journal." Get a notebook with tabs. Divide the journal into subject headings. Every time a television show, magazine, friend, or co-worker sparks an idea, write it down under the appropriate heading. Multilevel classrooms require creative utilization of time, energy, and material resources. An idea journal can help tremendously.

17. Join some kind of group for recreational purposes. Doing something you love to do with others you find mutually satisfying is extremely important. The rest, relaxation, and fun are necessary for maintaining mental health. In addition, our hobbies can often be put to good use in the classroom to extend and enrich the curriculum.

18. Plan something positive for yourself each day. Take at least 30 minutes to do something enjoyable for yourself. Knowing that a reward is waiting after the paperwork is done also helps.

19. Take time regularly to assess progress and set new goals. Part of the job of avoiding burnout is feeling successful. Savor your successes to recharge your batteries. Then set new goals to feel successful again. Falling into a rut can be the worst kind of stress.

20. Join a professional organization such as the National Alliance for People with Mental Illness (NAMI), the Federation of Families, the Council for Exceptional Children (CEC), or one of the divisions of CEC such as the Council for Children with Behavioral Disorders (CCBD). These organizations use the power of numbers to advocate for youth with learning and behavior problems at the state and federal levels. In addition, these organizations provide much needed information on the latest research regarding youth with challenges, annual conference, support groups for families, and a collegial atmosphere that facilitates continued growth.

The Appendixes includes sample worksheets, progress charts, intervention strategies, and other information intended to make life in the classroom easier to organize and manage.

REFERENCES

Alberto, P. A. & Troutman, A. C. (1990). Applied behavior analysis for teachers: Influencing student performance, 5th edition. Columbus, OH: Charles E. Merrill Publishing Company.

Andrade, H. (2000). Using rubrics to promote thinking and learning. Educational Leadership, 57(5), 13-18.

Borkowski, J. (1992). Metacognitive theory: A framework for teaching literacy, writing, and math skills. Journal of Learning Disabilities, 25(4), 253-257.

Boudah, D., Lenz, B. K., Bulgren, J., Schumaker, J., & Deshler, D. (2000). Don't water down! Enhance content learning through the unit organizer routine. Teaching Exceptional Children, 32(3), 48-56.

Brandenburg, N. A., Friedman, J. M., & Silver, S. E. (1990). The epidemiology of childhood psychiatric disorders: Prevalence findings from recent studies. Journal of the American Academy of Child and Adolescent Psychiatry, 29, 76-83.

Burke, J. (1998). Decreasing classroom behavior problems: Practical guidelines for teachers. San Diego, CA: Singular.

Carney, R., Levin, M., & Levin, T. (1993). Mnemonic strategies: Instructional techniques worth remembering. Teaching Exceptional Children, 25(4), 24-30.

Chan, L. K., Cole, P. G., & Barfett, S. (1987). Comprehension monitoring: Detection and identification of text inconsistencies by LD and normal students. Learning Disability Quarterly, 10(2), 114-124.

Chan, L. K., Cole, P. G., & Morris, J. N. (1990). Effects of instruction in the use of visual-imagery strategy on the reading-comprehension competence of disabled and average readers. Learning Disability Quarterly, 13(1), 2-11.

Cohen, D., & Cohen, S. (2001, August 6). Census sees vast change in language, employment: More people work at home, more speak little English. The Washington Post, pp. A1, A5.

Cunningham, A. (1990). Explicit vs. implicit instruction in phonemic awareness. Journal of Experimental Child Psychology, 50, 429-444.

Deshler, D., & Schumaker, J. (1986). Learning strategies: An instructional alternative for low-achieving adolescents. Exceptional Children, 52, 583-590.

Deshler, D., Ellis, E., & Lenz, K. (1996). Teaching adolescents with learning disabilities, 2nd edition. Denver, CO: Love.

Dixon, R. (1994). Research synthesis in language arts: Curriculum guidelines for diverse learners. Monograph for the National Center to Improve Tools for Educators. Eugene, OR: University of Oregon.

Dixon, R., Carnine, D. & Kameenui, E. (1992). Research synthesis in mathematics: Curriculum guidelines for diverse learners. Monograph for the National Center to Improve the Tools of Educators. Eugene, OR: University of Oregon.

Dixon, Carnine, Lee, Wallin, & Chard (1998).

Driekurs, R., Grunwald, B., & Pepper, F. (1982). Maintaining sanity in the classroom. New York: Harper and Row.

Edmunds, A. (1999). Cognitive credit cards: Acquiring learning strategies. Teaching Exceptional Children, 31(4), 68-73.

Frender, G. (1990). Learning to learn. Nashville, TN: Incentive Publications.

Forness, S., & Kavale, K. (2002). Defining emotional or behavioral disorders in school and related services. In J. Lloyd, E. Kameenui, & D. Chard (Eds.), Issues in educating students with disabilities (pp. 45-61). Mahwah, NJ: Erlbaum.

Fujiura, G. T., & Yamaki, K. (2000).

Glasser, W. (1985). Control theory in the classroom. New York: Harper Perennial.

Glasser, W. (1998). Choice theory. New York: Harper Perennial.

Grossen, B., & Lee, C. (1994). Research synthesis in science: Curriculum guidelines for diverse learners. Monograph for the National Center to Improve the Tools of Educators. Eugene, OR: University of Oregon.

Guetzloe, E. C. (1989). Youth suicide: What the educator should know. Reston, VA: Council for Exceptional Children.

Hall, T. (2002a). Explicit instruction: Effective classroom practices report. National Center on Accessing the General Curriculum. Available at http://www.ncac.org

Hall, T. (2002b). Differentiated instruction: Effective classroom practices report. National Center on Accessing the Curriculum. Available at http://www.ncac.org

Hesley, J. W., & Hesley, J. G. (1998). Rent two movies and let's talk in the morning. New York, NY: John Wiley & Sons, Inc.

Harris, K., & Pressley, M. (1991). The nature of cognitive strategy instruction: Interactive strategy construction. Exceptional Children, 57(5), 392-404.

Heward, W., Gardner III, R., Cavanaugh, R., Courson, F., Grossi, T., & Barbetta, P. (1996). Everyone participates in this class. Teaching Exceptional Children, 28(2), 4-10.

Hurford, D. P., Darrow, L. J., Edwards, T. L., Howerton, C. J., Mote, C. R., Schauf, J. D., & Coffey, P. (1993). An examination of phonemic processing abilities in children during their first-grade year. Journal of Learning Disabilities, 26(3), 167-177.

Hyerle, D. (1996). Visual tools for constructing knowledge. Alexandria, VA: ASCD.

Joint Committee on Teacher Planning for Students with Disabilities (1995). Planning for academic diversity in america's classrooms: Windows on reality, research, change, and practice. Lawrence, KS: University of Kansas.

Kauffman, J. (2001). Characteristics of emotional and behavioral disorders of children and youth (7th ed.). Upper Saddle River, NJ: Merrill Prentice-Hall.

Kameenui, E., & Carnine, D. (1998). Effective teaching strategies that accommodate diverse learners. Upper Saddle River, NJ: Prentice Hall.

Kameenui, E., Simmons, D., Baker, S., Chard, D., Dickson, S., Gunn, B., Lin, S.-J., Smith, S., & Sprick, M. (1994). Research synthesis in early reading and literacy: Curriculum guidelines for diverse learners. Monograph for the National Center to Improve Tools for Educators. Eugene, OR: University of Oregon.

Katz, M. (1997). On playing a poor hand well: Insights from the lives of those who have overcome childhood risks and adversities. New York, NY: W. W. Norton.

Koplewicz, H. (1996). It's nobody's fault: New hope and help for difficult children. New York, NY: Three Rivers Press.

Larkin, M. (2001). Providing support for student independence through scaffolded instruction. Teaching Exceptional Children, 34(1), 30-34.

Miller, S., Crawford, D., Harness, M., & Hollenbeck, K. (1994). Research synthesis in social studies: Curriculum guidelines for diverse learners. Monograph for the National Center to Improve Tools for Educators. Eugene, OR: University of Oregon.

Kidder, R., & Born, P. (1999). Resolving ethical dilemmas in the classroom. Educational Leadership, 56(4), 38-41.

Knoff, H. (2000). Stop and think! Steps toward the systematic prevention of student violence. Reaching Today's Youth, 5(1), 63-66.

Kupper, L. (1994). (Ed.). A guide to children's literature and disability. Washington, D. C.: NICHCY.

Lewis, T. J., & Sugai, G. (1999). Effective behavior support: A systems approach to proactive schoolwide management. Focus on Exceptional Children, 31(6), 1-24.

Malone, L., & Mastropieri, M. (1992). Reading comprehension instruction: Summarization and self-monitoring training for students with learning disabilities. Exceptional Children, 58(3), 270-279.

McClanahan, E., & Wicks, C. (1993). Future force: Kids that want to, can, and do! Chino Hills, CA: PACT Publishing.

Office of Special Education Programs (1996). Learning to read. Reading to learn. Washington, D. C.: U. S. Department of Education.

O'Shea, D. J., O'Shea, L. J., Algozinne, R., & Hammittee, D. J. (Eds.). (2001). Families and teachers of individuals with disabilities: Collaborative orientations and responsive practices. Boston, MA: Allyn & Bacon.

Prater, M. A. (1999). Characterization of mental retardation in children's and adolescent literature. Education and Training in Mental Retardation and Developmental Disabilities, 34(4), 418-431.

Pressley, M., Borkowski, J., & Schneider, W. (1989). Good information processing: What it is and what education can do to promote it. International Journal of Educational Research, 13, 857-867.

Prelutsky, J. (1984). The new kid on the block. New York, NY: Greenwillow Books.

Redl, F. (1966). When we deal with children. New York: Free Press.

Sugai, G., Horner, R., Dunlap, G., Scott, T., Liaupsin, C., Sailor, W., Turnbull, A., Turnbull, H., Wickham, D., Wilcox, B. (2000). Applying positive support and functional behavioral assessment in schools. Journal of Positive Behavior Interventions, 2, 131-143.

Schunk, D., & Rice, J. (1992). Influence of reading comprehension strategy information on children's achievement outcomes. Learning Disability Quarterly, 15(4), 51-64.

Scott, R. M., & Nelson, C. M., (1999). Functional behavioral assessment: Implications for training and staff development. Behavioral Disorders, 24, 70-84.

Shure, A., Morocco, C., DiGisi, L., & Yenkin, L. (1999). Pathways to planning: Improving student achievement in inclusive classrooms. Teaching Exceptional Children, 32(1), 54.

Shure, M. (1992). I can problem solve: An interpersonal cognitive problem solving program. Champaign, IL: Research Press.

Scott, T. M. (2001). A school-wide example of positive behavior support. Journal of Positive Behavior Interventions, 3(2), 88-94.

Simmonds, E. P. (1990). The effectiveness of two methods for teaching a constraint-seeking questioning strategy to students with learning disabilities. Journal of Learning Disabilities, 23(4), 229-233.

Sprick, R., Sprick, M., & Garrison, M. (1992). Foundations: Developing positive school-wide discipline policies. Longmont, CO: Sopris West.

Stoodt-Hill, B., & Amspaugh-Corson, L. (2001). Children's literature: Discovery for a lifetime, 2nd ed. Upper Saddle River, NJ: Merrill Prentice-Hall.

Swanson, H. L. (1989). Strategy instruction: Overview of principles and procedures for effective use. Learning Disability Quarterly, 12(1), 3-14.

Tomlinson, C. (1999, October). The differentiated classroom: Responding to the needs of all learners. The School Administrator, 56, 6-11.

U. S. Department of Health and Human Services (2001). Report of the Surgeon's General's Conference on Children's Mental Health: A National Action Agenda. Washington D. C.: Author.

Wasta, S., Scott, M., Marchand-Martella, N., & Harris, R. (1999). From the great wall to a great inclusive classroom: Integrated instruction at work. Teaching Exceptional Children, 31(6), 60-65.

Wong, B. Y., & Wong, R. (1989). Study behavior as a function of metacognitive knowledge about critical task variables: An investigation of above average, average, and learning disabled readers. Learning Disabilities Research, 1(2), 101-111.

Appendix A

SAMPLE LESSON PLAN FORMS

Lesson planning can be streamlined to take minimum time for maximum benefit. Within the first month of a school year, a master copy can be developed with blanks left for page numbers, instructional techniques, and evaluation methods. The master copy can include the following:

1. Teacher's name
2. Names of students in each instructional group
3. Times for each activity
4. Textbook titles
5. Subject headings
6. Instructions for daily and weekly events

A page of abbreviations should be stapled to the front of the lesson plan book or weekly forms. Multiple copies of these can be made and filed for future use along with copies of the master form. Sample copies of an abbreviation list and a master lesson plan form follow. Lesson planning time can be reduced to 60 to 90 minutes per week using this method. Another time saver is arranging material to be covered in units. If textbook or student groups change, erase incorrect information and add the new information. Use a highlighting pen on the most important information. This can be a big help when things get hectic.

ABBREVIATIONS LIST FOR LESSON PLANS

Act	Activities
DOM	Daily Oral Math
DOW	Daily Oral Writing
DVE	Daily Vocabulary Enrichment
Eval	Evaluation Procedure
IP	Independent Practice
p, pp	Page number, page numbers
Sp	Spelling
SP	Student Product
TDL	Teacher Directed Lesson
TM	Teacher's Manual
TMM	Teacher-made Materials
TO	Teacher Observation
TT	Timed Test
w/	With
wds	Words
wksht	Worksheet
w/o	Without

SAMPLE LESSON PLAN FORMAT

_____ Week of _____ Subject _____ Time _____
    (Teacher)

Group I. _____ Book _____
               (Students' Names)

Group II. _____ Book _____
              (Students' Names)

Daily Activities
    TT on individual facts
    DOM found in book _____ on p _____

Monday: **Group I.** Obj _____
           TDL/TM p _____   Assignment p. _____
           Eval _____
           Group II. Obj _____
           TDL/TM p _____   Assignment p. _____
           Eval _____

Tuesday: **Group I.** Obj _____
           TDL/TM p _____   Assignment p. _____
           Eval _____
           Group II. Obj _____
           TDL/TM p _____   Assignment p. _____
           Eval _____

Wednesday: **Group I.** Obj _____
           TDL/TM p _____   Assignment p. _____
           Eval _____
           Group II. Obj _____
           TDL/TM p _____   Assignment p. _____
           Eval _____

Thursday: **Group I.** Obj _____
           TDL/TM p _____   Assignment p. _____
           Eval _____
           Group II. Obj _____
           TDL/TM p _____   Assignment p. _____
           Eval _____

Friday: **Group I.** Obj _____
           TDL/TM p _____   Assignment p. _____
           Eval _____
           Group II. Obj _____
           TDL/TM p _____   Assignment p. _____
           Eval _____

Appendix B

SAMPLE WORKSHEETS

The following worksheet ideas can help decrease behavior problems by providing alternative methods of practicing similar skills. The same skill to be reinforced is shown in each example to illustrate various ways one skill might be practiced. The skill illustrated in the examples is distinguishing short a and short i vowel sounds. This is a primary skill. The worksheet ideas, however, are adaptable to more sophisticated skills.

FOR STUDENTS WHO HATE TO WRITE

Cut and Paste Activities

Provide worksheets with a word or letter bank. The students cut the correct answer from the bank and paste it in the appropriate space on the worksheet. Older students might prefer to cut words or letters from old magazines or newspapers.

1. The _____ can fly.

2. Jan will _____ on the mat.

3. The dog and _____ can run.

4. The hat _____ Dad.

Word Bank
cat
sit
bat
fits

1. Put the ham in the p__n.

2. The bat h__t the ball.

3. P__t the cat on the head.

Letter Bank
a   i

a   i

a   i

Matching Worksheets

The student can draw a line or glue yarn to match items with correct answers.

1. The _____ is brown.

2. The _____ can fly

3. The dog and _____ can run.

4. Jan will _____ on the mat.

5. The hat _____ Dad.

Word Bank
cat
fits
sit
bat
mitt

Trace Stencils

Students who hate to write often enjoy tracing stencils. An answer sheet will need to be provided with spaces big enough to accommodate stenciled responses. Decorating the answers when time permits is a common source of enjoyment.

Circle Correct Answers/Multiple Choice

For each item, give two to four possible responses under or beside the question. The student circles the correct answers or puts a code letter for the correct answer in the appropriate space.

Circle one correct answer for each sentence.

1. The _____ is brown.   sit   mitt

2. The _____ can fly.   cat   bat

3. The dog and _____ can run.   fits   cat

4. Jan will _____ on the mat.   sit   mitt

FOR STUDENTS WHO HATE MATH

Students who hate math usually have a great deal of difficulty with new concepts. Move slowly. Provide plenty of practice with hands-on materials. Divide worksheets into two or more parts. The student can be given small rewards for each part completed. Math puzzles that require coloring or assembly are also motivating. The progress charts in the next section may help these students.

At the beginning of the year provide everyone with a math folder. These can be quick references for the students to use unless they are told that the assignment has been designed to assess their mastery of those skills and facts. The folders can include math terms and their definitions, a laminated number line, a place values chart, measurement equivalents, and step-by-step procedures to follow for word problems and other multi-step computations they will need to know. Concept development is often hindered by poor vocabulary. A sixth grade student who still gets confused during a math lesson unless the teacher says 'take away' instead of subtraction may need to spend time learning math terms. Informally assess students' vocabulary understanding as well as their computational skills.

WORK SIGN-OFF SHEET

Name _____   **Week of** _____

(Place subjects, activities, &/or times in this column.)	**Monday**	**Tuesday**	**Wednesday**	**Thursday**	**Friday**

Target Behavior(s)

_____

_____

_____

Number of Sign-offs Needed to Earn the Friday Activity

_____

Appendix C

SAMPLE PROGRESS CHARTS

The following progress charts provide various ways for students to keep track of their achievements. Students need concrete evidence of their past successes. Having a record of their accomplishments is a positive way to keep them motivated.

Skills Checklist

Name _____

School Year _____

Age _____ DOB _____

READING

Sight Word Recognition

A check indicates 85% or higher accuracy on an oral test of Harris Jacobson sight words read in isolation.

Set	1	2	3	4	5	6	7	8	9	10	11	12	13	14	15
First															
Second															
Third															
Fourth															
Fifth															

Phonics

Initial Consonant Sounds

B C D F G H J K L M N P Q R S T V W X Y Z

Final Consonant Sounds

B C D F G H J K L M N P Q R S T V W X Y Z

Short Vowels   A E I O U

Long Vowels   A E I O U

Blends and Diagraphs

th   sh   wh

bl   cl   fl   gl   pl   sl

br   cr   dr   fr   fr   pr   sr   tr

st   str   spr

COMPREHENSION

Type of test used _____

A check indicates 85% or higher accuracy.

Question Type	P	1	2	3	4	5	Comments
Detail							
Main Idea							
Inference							
Drawing Conclusions							

MATH

Numeration

Oral counting from 0 to:

___10 ___20 ___30 ___40 ___50 ___60 ___70 ___80 ___90 ___100

Skip counting by   ___2s   ___5s   ___10s

Recognition of written numerals from 0 to

___10 ___20 ___30 ___40 ___50 ___60 ___70 ___80 ___90 ___100
___150 ___500 ___1,000 ___2,000 ___10,000 ___100,000

MATH FACTS

A check indicates 85% accuracy or higher

	0	1	2	3	4	5	6	7	8	9	10
Addition											
Subtraction											
Multiplication											
Division											

OTHER SKILLS

Word Problems   Grade Levels: 1   2   3   4   5   6

___ Oral counting by 2s
___ Oral counting by 5s
___ Oral counting by 10s
___ Regrouping—Addition
___ Regrouping—Subtraction
___ Two-digit Multiplication

___ Two-digit Division
___ Makes change to $1.00
___ Makes change to $5.00
___ Linear Measurement
___ Liquid Measurement (volume)
___ Shapes

Language
___ Capitalizes proper nouns
___ Capitalizes initial words in a sentence
___ Capitalizes the personal pronoun "I"
___ Uses periods
___ Uses questions marks
___ Uses exclamation points
___ Uses synonyms
___ Uses antonyms
___ Uses homophones
___ Alphabetizes to the first letter
___ Alphabetizes to the second letter
___ Alphabetizes to the third letter
___ Uses commas in dates
___ Uses commas between words in a series
___ Uses commas between cities and states
___ Uses commas to set of expletives and antecedents
___ Composes a complete sentence
___ Writes three or more sentences in paragraph form
___ Writes two or more paragraphs in story or report form

SCIENCE UNITS

	Vocabulary	Concepts	Application
Human Body			
Animals			
Nutrition			
Plants			
Machines			
Magnets & Electricity			
Matter			
Space			
Weather			

SOCIAL STUDIES UNITS

	Vocabulary	Concepts	Application
Maps			
American History			
Other Cultures			
Holidays			
Economics			
Current Events			
Government			
Community Helpers			
Your State			

GRAPH OF TEST SCORES

Name _____

Starting Date _____

Mastery Date _____

Skill Set _____

Math facts or vocabulary can be placed in the "Items to Be Mastered" section. Periodic test scores can be recorded on the graph.

Items to Be Mastered

1. 25						
2. 24						
3. 23						
4. 22						
5. 21						
6. 20						
7. 19						
8. 18						
9. 17						
10. 16						
11. 15						
12. 14						
13. 13						
14. 12						
15. 11						
16. 10						
17. 9						
18. 8						
19. 7						
20. 6						
21. 5						
22. 4						
23. 3						
24. 2						
25. 1						
0						

Test Dates

Name _____   Date _____

Step Right Up!

Place the goal on the top of the ladder. Place the intermediate goals to reaching the goal on the steps of the ladders. The student can color the steps of the ladder or place a sticker on each step as the intermediate goal is mastered.

Name _____   Date _____

Leap to Your Goal!

Appendix D

SAMPLE NOTES TO AIDES

The following handouts are samples from my experience with aides in different school systems. Because each system has different criteria for hiring aides, their knowledge and skills can vary tremendously. These pages are meant to help the teacher begin thinking about the aide's role in the classroom. Providing the aide with a written list of classroom procedures before the children arrive can assist in building a productive team approach.

STUDENTS WITH BEHAVIOR PROBLEMS

Children with behavior disorders display a variety of characteristics. Typical behavior can include excessive use profanity, spitting, kicking, biting, scratching, hitting, teasing other children, refusing to follow directions, disrespectful behavior toward adults, destroying materials, stealing, and making annoying noises in many different ways.

The reasons for the behavior also vary. Some children have suffered abuse, neglect, or prenatal damage due to the mother's use of drugs during pregnancy. Others have neurological or chemical imbalances that contribute to their behavior problems. For some, the source of their difficulties is not clear. They are capable of learning. Our jobs is twofold:

1. To help them increase their ability to use self-control in maintaining appropriate school behavior.

2. To increase their academic skills to appropriate levels for their ages.

Please familiarize yourself with the Classroom Behavior Management Plan. Behavior modification techniques are based on learning theories and are designed to help the child achieve a positive sense of self-control. Results are often gradual. This is not a quick-fix method of control. The children are faced with choices and learn through positive reinforcement and punishments that they can control themselves.

The following dos and don'ts will make the day easier for you and the children.

Do

1. Compliment the children whenever possible for appropriate behavior and academic achievement.

2. Talk in a calm, even tone even if the child is upset or angry.

3. Notice small changes in behavior that might signal a possible problem. Talk to the child, make seating arrangements, or redirect an activity to help diffuse the situation.

4. Follow through on any directions or promises given to the children.

5. Remember that even when a child is acting disrespectfully toward you, it is not personal. The child is reacting to any number of past experiences. Staying calm and firmly in control of yourself will help the child.

6. Describe in clear, positive terms behavior you like, behavior you dislike, and behavior you expect.

7. Ignore, whenever possible, inappropriate behavior that is not dangerous.

8. Voice any concerns or disagreements with the discipline policy the teacher has established before the children arrive or after they have left. The children need to know that the adults in charge are mutually supportive. Failure to present a united front will encourage the children to try to weaken the rules by manipulating the adults into disagreements.

9. Ask for and take breaks when you need them.

Don't

1. Call the children names.

2. Overreact to their behavior by raising your voice unnecessarily.

3. Hit or spank the children.

4. Make threats.

5. Argue with the children.

6. Question the teacher's authority in front of the children.

MATERIALS MANAGEMENT

1. Bulletin boards are changed at the beginning of each month. Please assist the teacher with this duty. Materials are filed in large envelopes according to the month. File materials carefully and keep envelopes in order.

2. Homework folders will be made each month. We will construct the folders with the children. Please check the folders each morning as the children arrive. Record their performance on the chart provided. Assist the teacher in refilling the folders before the children go home each Monday through Thursday.

3. Work envelopes will be sent home every other Monday. Please count the papers in each student's work box. Stuff the envelopes, record the number of papers in each envelope on the front, and place the work envelopes with the homework folders.

4. Materials to be photocopied will be kept in a special box. Please put photocopied materials in the correct order and place master copies in the folders provided before returning the materials to the box.

5. Please assist the teacher and students in keeping all instructional kits, learning games, art materials, cooking supplies, and toys organized and in proper condition.

6. Assist the teacher with grading papers and recording grades.

7. Assist the teacher with filling out forms.

8. Our first priority is the students. Please don't worry about items 1 through 7 in this list at times when the students need your assistance.

INSTRUCTIONAL ASSISTANCE

1. While the teacher is teaching small groups, please be available to assist individual students with independent assignments. Assistance can include the following:
   a. Reading and explaining directions
   b. Helping a student sound out a word
   c. Giving a student additional clues through leading questions
   d. Providing the student with self-help materials such as counters, a dictionary, or picture clues
   e Offering encouragement and faith in the student's ability to complete the assignment

Please do not repeatedly give students answers, do parts of their work for them, or sit for long periods of time with one student. Independent work periods are intended to help students learn to use their time well and strengthen their problem-solving skills. Students need to strike a balance between receiving needed assistance and coming to depend too heavily on adult intervention.

2. If students complete independent work early, engage them in one of the following educational activities:
   a. Flashcard drill with sight words or math facts
   b. Board games using reading or math skills

      c. Listening to a student read a library book

      d. Playing "Hang-man" using reading or spelling vocabulary

      e. Oral drill of spelling words

3. During whole-group lessons, feel free to take a break, run off materials, or work on bulletin board materials.

Appendix E

SAMPLE NOTE TO PARENTS

Keeping parents informed is an important part of the job. With all the other paperwork a teacher has to do, time-saving techniques are a must.

For weekly or monthly good behavior notes, it is helpful to purchase books that contain preprinted and illustrated fill-in-the-blank style notes for photocopying. A few ideas follow. Homework folders and work envelopes can be run through a copying machine. Spaces for teacher and parent comments as well as the parent's signature can be printed directly on manila folders and large brown envelopes.

An introductory letter at the beginning of the year and a second semester information letter are teacher-made items that many parents appreciate.

Date_____

Dear_____

This is just to let you know
how proud we are of _____
for _____.

Thanks!

SAMPLE LETTER TO PARENTS

Date _____

Dear Parents,

Enclosed in this envelope are the following items:
A   Supply List
B. Word Cards
C. Math Cards
D. Game Board
E. _____
F. _____

The word cards, math cards, and game boards are for you and your child to use at home. Periodically, your child will bring home new sets of word and math fact cards as well as science and social studies information you can review. New game boards will also be sent home each month. Please do not return game boards and cards.

On Mondays through Thursdays your child will bring home a homework folder. Each evening there will be a math and a spelling assignment. Please check to make sure that your child does the homework and returns the folder each day. No homework will be assigned on holidays and Fridays.

I am looking forward to a productive year with your child. We will be involved in many interesting and challenging activities. Please call any time you have a question. The school's telephone number is _____. We are both interested in providing the best experience possible for your child. I welcome and appreciate your concern and cooperation.

Sincerely,

SUPPLY LIST

- Notebook Paper
- Scissors
- Pencils
- Glue Stick
- Erasers
- Tissues
- Colored Pencils or Marker
- Ruler

WORD CARDS

MATH FACTS CARDS

GAME BOARD

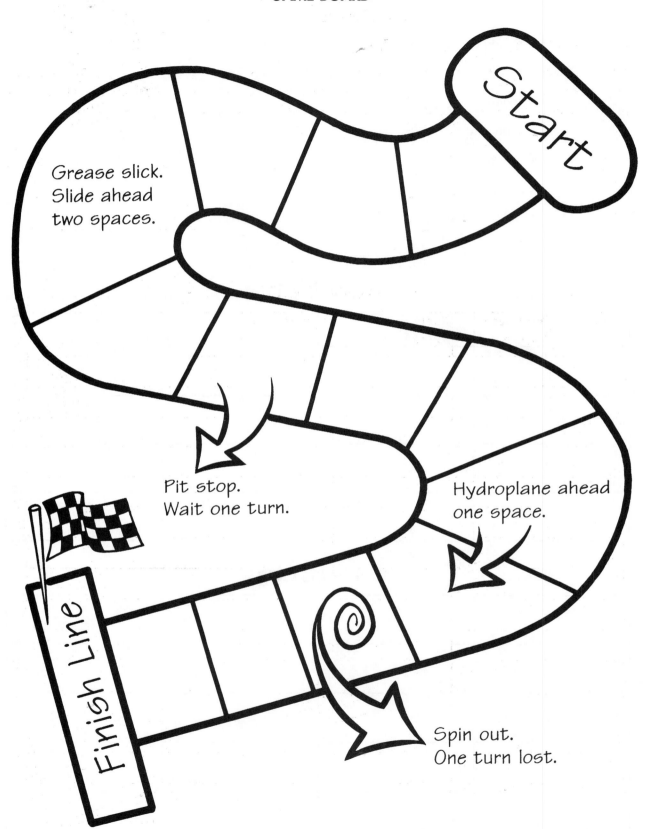

Start

Grease slick.
Slide ahead
two spaces.

Pit stop.
Wait one turn.

Hydroplane ahead
one space.

Finish Line

Spin out.
One turn lost.

WORK ENVELOPE

Dear Parents,

This envelope will be sent home every 2 weeks. Please look at _____'s work. Feel free to call me at _____ if you have questions or concerns. Your student needs to return the envelope with your signature on it each time it is sent home.

Thank you!

_____

INFORMATION LETTER

Date	Number of Papers	Parent's Signature	Comments

PROJECTED YEARLY GOALS

READING

Each child will proceed at his or her own pace in reading. Instruction will include four areas of emphasis.

A. Harris Jacobson sight word drills will be conducted daily using flashcards and a variety of teacher-made games and worksheets.

B. Phonics instruction will include initial and final consonants, long and short vowels, and blends and diagraphs.

C. Comprehension skills instruction will include the use of pictures, discussions, worksheets, and basal materials to emphasize the recall of detail, the ability to make inferences, and the skill of drawing conclusions.

D. To foster and appreciation of reading, weekly trips to the library, daily story time periods, and an opportunity to earn free reading periods will be provided by the teacher.

MATH

Each child will proceed at his or her own pace in math instruction through the basal materials provided by the schools. Instruction will center on the following activities:

A. Daily drill in numeration skills as well as math facts using flashcards, oral patterning, and games.

B. Written work in workbooks, on worksheets, or with the math kit.

C. Hands-on problem-solving experiences using, for example, art, building activities, or cooking.

LANGUAGE

Language instruction for each child will depend upon his or her reading level. Instruction in language will revolve around two broad area:

A. Oral Language Development:

This will include oral activities to stimulate the use of description, complete sentences, and sequencing when speaking as well as learning about synonyms, antonyms, and homonyms.

B. Written Language:

This will include punctuation; capitalization; grammar; parts of speech; and correct forms for writing sentences, paragraphs, and stories.

SPELLING

Spelling words for each child will be selected from reading and phonics patterns the child is learning in an effort to reinforce all three areas of instruction.

SCIENCE AND SOCIAL STUDIES

The following units are projected for the year:

Month	Science	Social Studies
August/September	Human Body	Maps
October	Animals	Settlers
November	Nutrition	Indians
December	Plants	Holidays
January	Machines	Japan
February	Magnets & Electricity	France
March	Matter	Economics
April	Space	Community Helpers
May	Weather	State History

Appendix F

SAMPLE DECISION-MAKING SHEET

Students who are unwilling or unable for some reason to discuss a problem can fill out a decision-making sheet. Simple sheets would include short, low-level vocabulary questions followed by one-or-two word multiple choice answers or pictures that can be circled. Older, more capable students can answer a more demanding questionnaire. A sample follows. Take time to read and discuss the student's responses with the student after it is complete. Make it clear that one mistake does not have to ruin the day or week.

THINK SHEET

Name _____ **Date** _____

1. **What was happening just before the problem occurred?** _____

_____

2. **What was the problem?** _____

_____

3. **What did you do?** _____

4. **How did you feel?** _____

5. **List at least 4 things you could have done to avoid or solve the problem.**

_____

_____

_____

_____

6. **Put a star next to the best choice from the 4 you listed in question 5.**

7. **What will you earn if you pick the choice you marked with a star?** _____

_____

8. **How will you reward yourself when you make a good choice the next time?**

_____

9. **How do you feel now?** _____

10. **How can you help yourself have a good day now that the problem is over?**

_____

Appendix G

SAMPLE INSTRUCTIONAL GAMES

Because of the children's low tolerance for frustration, material needs to be presented and practiced in a variety of ways. Children will balk at doing the same worksheet over and over, no matter how much they need the practice. Games used along with direct instruction and practice worksheets will speed the academic process and reduce stress for the students.

QUIZ SHOW TYPE GAMES

Write each student's initials on the chalkboard. Ask questions based on science, social studies, math, or any other academic subject. Stick to questions that can be answered with one or two words. Keep the questions moving quickly. Two points can be awarded for a correct response. One point can be awarded if the student tries but answers incorrectly. Erase a point for talk-outs. Earned points may be added to the bonus point balance, or they may be cashed in immediately following the game for small prizes.

Another way to do this is to ask questions that have only a few possible answers.Identifying exclamatory, declarative, and interrogative sentences can be done by giving each student three cards. Have the students draw a large period on one card, a large exclamation point on the second card, and a large question mark on the third card. As the teacher reads sentences, students can hold up the card that has the correct punctuation mark on it. For science, cards with animal group names can be given to each student. As characteristics and representative animals are presented, students hold up the card with the correct animal group name on it.

A third format includes the use of a tri-fold project board. Brightly colored library card pockets can be placed on the board with point values printed in large numbers on the pockets. Sentence strip tag board can be placed on the left margin to designate categories of questions. The pockets should be arranged in rows of increasing point values across categories. Students can be asked to compose 2-3 questions on an assigned topic. One question should be written on each 3" x 5" card. The students should write the answer to each question on the back of each card. The teacher reads the questions, assigns point values based on the difficulty level of the question, sorts the questions, discards duplicate questions, and composes additional questions to fill gaps in the content and/or point values. I usually assign the lowest number of points for simple recall questions. Comprehension, application, evaluation, and synthesis questions earn increasing numbers of points. Along the right margin of the project board, I place additional pockets for team names. These pockets hold the cards that teams answer correctly until the end of the game. Placing correctly answered questions in the corresponding team pocket makes keeping track of team responses easier and keeps teams from focusing on points alone during the game. Teams that talk loud enough during the game to distract other teams or interrupt the flow of the game forfeit a turn.

The Quiz Show

Category Title	50	100	150	Team Points
Category Title	50	100	150	Team Points
Category Title	50	100	150	Team Points

A Note About Prizes: Students should be encouraged to compete for their own reward rather than to beat another student or team. To accomplish this objective, establish rewards in graduated levels prior to playing the games. All students who attain a particular level of points in a game will earn the same reward. Examples of this strategy in action would include the following:

1. For every two points students earn in the chalkboard game, they can have a mini-marshmallow at the end of the game.
2. For every two correct responses with the cards, students can have 1 minute of earned time at the activity center.
3. Teams that earn 500—700 points may purchase a juice and a granola bar.
   Teams that earn 300—499 points may purchase a juice.
   Teams that earn 100—299 points may earn a granola bar.

BOARD GAMES

Board games can be made out of manila folders. Holiday themes, seasonal themes, and current super heroes can easily be incorporated into the game board illustrations by cutting pictures from magazines, newspapers, or gift wrap.

Students can use their own sight word cards or math facts. Games can be made with questions from science, social studies, or some other academic content area. These games can also be copied and sent home with the students. A simple spinner can be made from cardboard and a brass brad (paper fastener), or dice can be used. After so many years in the classroom, I have learned to use many items that others throw away as a cost-saving strategy. Large dice made from large sponges or empty milk or juice containers are a safe and inexpensive alternative to dice purchased at the store.

Board games are a wonderful way to fill those few minutes two or three students may have between assignments or other scheduled activities. They will need adult supervision to maintain appropriate behavior while playing.

A few examples of game boards are shown on the next few pages.

ACTION GAMES

These games allow the children to move around a little while practicing skills. Bean bag games, floor mats made of large pieces of cardboard or old sheets, cubes with numbers or letters printed on them, and 'eraser tag' games can all be adapted to practice a variety of academic skills.

CUBE GAMES

To make the cubes, cut the triangular tops off milk cartons. Cut the milk cartons to a height equal to the width of the cartons. Force one carton into the other carton. Cover the cube with paper. Print consonants, consonant blends, vowels, punctuation marks, or numbers on the cubes. Have the students roll the cubes to play the games. Two or three cubes with numbers on them can be rolled and arranged to form the highest or lowest number possible. The digits on the cubes can be added, subtracted, or multiplied. Cubes with letters can be used to practice initial, final, and medial consonant sounds; vowel sounds; and words with blends, diagraphs, suffixes, or prefixes. Cubes with punctuation marks can be used to initiate the generation of sentences that require the symbol shown on the upper horizontal plane of the cube.

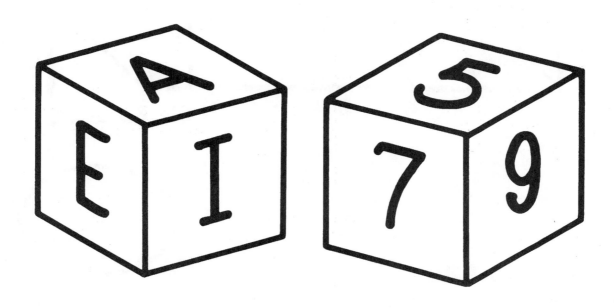

BOARD GAME

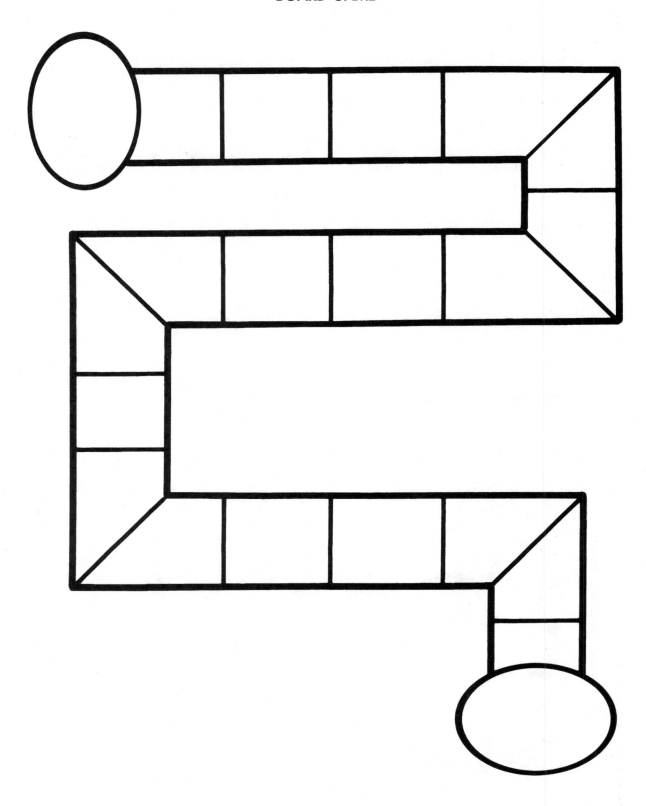

BEAN BAG GAMES

A cardboard box or large sheet of heavy cardboard from a packing crate can be used to make seasonal bean bag game boards. Cut the openings in the cardboard large enough to allow the bean bag to go through the opening. Numbers or letters can be placed at each opening. Students can generate words that contain the letters or practice math facts with the numbers.

Mats made of poster board or old sheets.

2	4	1
8	0	6
5	7	3

C	F	N	T
D	R	S	J
B	Qu	M	K
G	V	H	W

WORD PROBLEM MAP

What is the goal of the problem?	*Problem:* *Goal:*
Draw a picture to illustrate the problem.	
Select the necessary informa-tion.	
Decide operation(s).	
Compute Add, Subtract, Multiply, Divide	

STORY MAP

What is the setting of the story?	
Who are the important characters? **How are they related?**	
What is the problem?	
What are 3 important events that occur in the story?	
How is the problem solved?	

Appendix H

SAMPLE ORGANIZATIONAL PROJECTS FOR STUDENTS

Help students stay organized by making items in class that will encourage self-management. Homework folders, bank or pencil box decorations, school and classroom maps, student work boxes, and personal bulletin boards for class work and art work are some of the ideas students respond to positively.

HOMEWORK FOLDERS

Homework folders can be made from manila folders. Two inside pockets for homework and important notes can be made by having the students color a seasonal symbol or personal design. Glue the outer edges of the pictures to the inside of the folder. Put one picture on each side. Cover the whole inside with clear adhesive plastic. Carefully cut slits in the tips of the pictures without cutting through the folder itself. This forms the pockets. Put a chart on the back to record homework completion for the current grading period. The student can decorate the front.

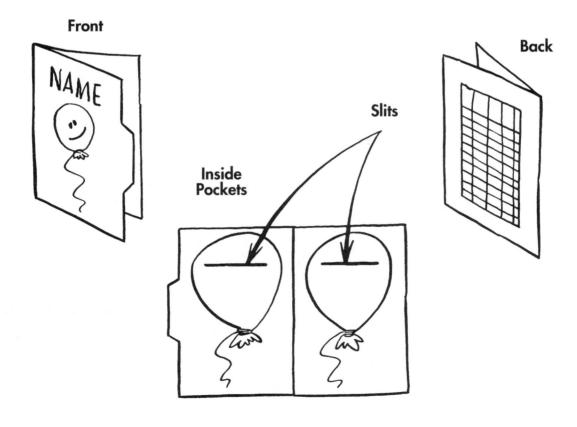

BANK OR PENCIL BOX DECORATIONS

If the classroom behavior management plan includes token of some kind, the students will need something in which to keep the tokens. Very young children who may be too distracted by a box on the desk may do better with a bag or envelope that hangs from the back of the chair or the side of the desk. Older children often like to have a small box on the desk. These boxes can also be used for pencils and crayons. An inexpensive way to make them is to cut the triangular tops off milk cartons, cover the sides with paper, and let the students decorate the boxes with holiday symbols, their names, or any other appropriate symbol. Preprinted patterns can also be purchased. This can become a monthly project along with calendar construction as a way to emphasize seasonal events, months of the year, and other related academic content.

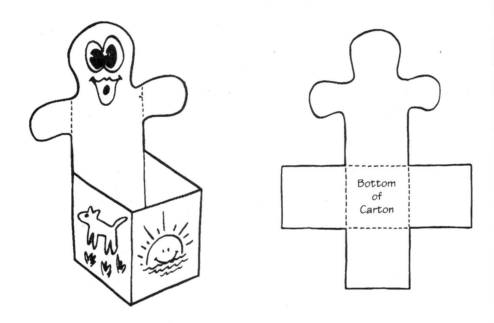

CLASSROOM AND SCHOOL MAPS

At the beginning of the school year, the class will need to be oriented to the class and school setting. This can be done during the social studies period by incorporating map skills into the lessons. Students can develop a classroom map first, complete with directional symbols and a key. A school map can then be developed. It is best to provide students with a basic floor plan to start. An outline of the room with windows and doors already printed can help them get started. Likewise, when beginning the map of the school, provide a preprinted outline of the whole school. Students can then take a walk to find out the names of the teachers and offices on the outline. These maps can be used to help new students later in the year.

WORK BOXES AND WORK ENVELOPES

Students will need a place to keep completed and graded papers. A file folder will work, but a box is especially useful because each student can then have two or three file folders along with the work envelope. This keeps materials together and provides the student with a place to keep things that others will not be permitted to touch. The file folders in the students' work boxes can include completed and graded work, incomplete work, and make-up work.

Cardboard flats cut from soda cases obtained from the grocery store are a good size. Large cereal or powdered detergent boxes also work nicely. Cover these with colored adhesive plastic. Put a student's name on each one and place the folders and work envelopes inside. Students may prefer to paint the boxes or decorate them with stickers.

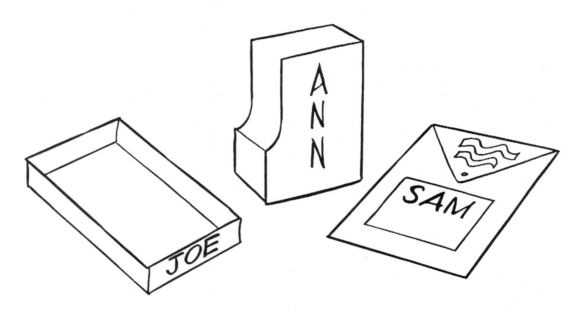

PERSONAL BULLETIN BOARDS

In some rooms bulletin board space is limited. To allow each student to have a place to display his or her work, make mini-bulletin boards out of heavy cardboard. Large, heavy cardboard boxes can be cut to any size desired. Cover the cardboard with spray paint, colored adhesive plastic, gift wrap, or construction paper. Let the students make borders for their own boards. Because tacks and push pins sometimes become weapons, large clips or painted clothes pins might be better for securing work to be displayed. Place holes in the top right and top left corners. Thread yarn through the holes. Hang the mini-bulletin boards from windows, ceiling tile frames, or hooks placed on the wall.

Another multipurpose display idea includes painting the backs of wooden clip boards with chalkboard paint for use at students' desks during math and spelling drills. When the lap chalkboards are not in use, students can display good work on the clip board as it hangs from a hook on the wall.

Appendix I

SAMPLE INTERVENTIONS

TEACHING DESIRED BEHAVIORS

Some students exhibit inappropriate behaviors because they have never learned the skills necessary for successful school participation. Other students know how to exhibit desired skills but have not had those behaviors reinforced with enough intensity or frequency to encourage them to continue to behave appropriately. Students should be given multiple opportunities to learn desired behaviors and have those behaviors recognized and rewarded. The following strategies can be used to teach and reinforce school appropriate behavior.

DESK POCKET FOR RESPONSE STRIPS

Some students exhibit mild behavior problems such as talking without permission or leaving their assigned areas with a frequency that creates unacceptable levels of disruption. Select a specific target behavior for an individual student and count the number of times the student exhibits that behavior in a specific period of time. This number represents baseline for that behavior. Place a strip of paper in a pocket at the front corner of the student's desk or on an easily accessible bulletin board. Explain to the student that a strip of paper will be pulled from the envelope each time the target behavior is exhibited. If the student has one or more strips of paper left in a given period of time, the student will be able to trade the remaining strip or strips for a predetermined reinforcer. As the student exhibits fewer occurrences of the target behavior, fewer strips should be put in the pocket. If a student destroys the pocket or strips, the student should pay points to have the pocket and strips replaced. Time will start over.

BEHAVIOR BINGO

Behavior Bingo is a positive way to teach and reinforce desired behaviors. Provide each of the students with a blank Bingo grid and a page of Bingo words and icons. The students can cut the words and icons apart and glue them into the squares of the blank grid to create their own Bingo board. The numbers in the example that follows represent the classroom rules that are posted and illustrated. The other items represent problem-solving and active listening steps. After teaching the skills through discussion, role play, and response card games, play Behavior Bingo. These Bingo boards can be placed in the Substitute Folder for the substitute to use in reviewing rules and procedures on days that the teacher is absent.

Note: The Stop, Think, Act, Review (STAR) strategy for self-management is taken from the work of Howard Knoff (2000) and is incorporated into the overall behavior management program for students in my class. Students who make good choices earn rewards. Students who make bad choices earn punishments and/or educative interventions designed to teach desired behaviors.

BEHAVIOR BINGO

STOP	THINK	ACT	REVIEW
C GOOD CHOICE	**D** BAD CHOICE	**1**	**2**
3	**4**	**5**	ASK QUESTIONS
SIT UP	LEAN FORWARD	**J** BAD CHOICE	TRACK THE SPEAKER

WRITING ASSIGNMENTS

Some people object to having students write as a consequence for inappropriate behavior.

The concern is that students will have negative feelings about all writing activities if some writing activities are associated with punishment. That has not been my experience. Students, like their teachers, make a distinction between boring paperwork and creative, rewarding experiences.

Writing assignments can sometimes help students focus on specific behaviors in ways that other activities do not. When students write as a consequence for inappropriate behavior, care must be taken to make the assignment appropriate for the age and ability level of the student. Problems-solving or decision-making sheets are one example. Having a student copy particular rules and write about the reasons for these rules is another example.

With extreme problems that do not respond to other methods, such as nonstop sex talk, a longer writing assignment focusing not only on the school consequences for such behavior, but also on the greater life problems that the behavior can create has worked well with older, middle school students. The longer examples are not recommended for elementary level students or students who, due to severe psychosis, may not be aware of everything they do.

On more than one occasion, these writing assignments have dramatically reduced the behavior described in them. Students have told me after copying a particular paragraph that they never realized until they wrote the assigned passage how much trouble their behavior could cause them. Only one student has had to copy an assignment more than once. That student needed only two experiences with one of the assignments to reduce the inappropriate responses from as many as 13 per 15 minute time periods to 2 or 3 occurrences per day. Eventually, using other methods, the student completely stopped making the inappropriate responses in the classroom. Some examples of these writing assignments follow.

SAMPLE WRITING ASSIGNMENT A: SEX TALK

When I make sexually inappropriate remarks and gestures with my body, I make myself look bad. Others may feel shocked, sick, or bored. No matter how they feel, they can see that my attitude about an adult subject is very immature. As I become interested in dating, I realize that my comments will cause girls to stay away from me. Other guys will not want to be around me or double date with me, because my comments and actions will embarrass them in front of their girlfriends. As I move into the workplace, my comments will hurt my chances of getting and keeping a good job. Bosses will not appreciate rude comments—especially in front of customers. It is definitely in my best interest to keep sexually inappropriate comments and gestures to myself. If I do, I will increase my ability to impress others with my maturity, make friends more easily, and find better employment.

SAMPLE WRITING ASSIGNMENT B: RESPONDING APPROPRIATELY

When I make inappropriate comments and respond to the inappropriate behavior of others, several things happen. I interrupt classmates and teachers who have work to do. I encourage friends to do and say things that will get them in trouble. I allow myself to continue a habit that is destructive to me. I may get a brief feeling of pleasure out of the attention I get, but in the end, I feel very uncomfortable. The people who laugh at me end up with consequences also. This interferes with my ability to make real friends. This behavior interferes with classroom procedures. And worst of all, this behavior interferes with my own growth.

I am an intelligent person. I have good ideas and am capable of finding conversation topics that interest me and others without being disruptive and inappropriate. I am also a caring person. I care about my classmates and how my example affects them. I also care about my own growth and maturity.

In order for me to continue the progress I am making, I need to talk less and think more for a while. I need to evaluate myself before I speak or laugh. Are my words helpful? Could someone misunderstand me because of my actions? Do I want the privileges I can earn by showing others more responsible behavior? Will I feel better about myself after I speak? Is it appropriate to laugh or talk now? Will this help my friends?

After I take time to evaluate my actions, I am sure I can make good choices. Others will know I have grown. I will be recognized as a leader. I can look forward to a better education, more friends, more self-confidence, a better job, and a greater feeling of accomplishment.

Learning new skills and habits is never easy. This will require a great deal of effort and concentration. But, I have accomplished other difficult things. With time, hard work, and perseverance, I can accomplish the goals of talking appropriately and ignoring the inappropriate behavior of peers. I want to do this partly to avoid the consequences I get when I don't. I want to do this partly to earn the rewards, friends, and inner feelings of pride and self-confidence that greater self-control and maturity provide.

SAMPLE WRITING ASSIGNMENT C: EXPRESSING ANGER

This type of writing assignment should be used with upper-elementary-aged students.

I have a responsibility to myself and others to express anger in ways that do not hurt people or destroy property. I can use words instead of actions. I can ask for help before things get too hard to handle. I can avoid some problems by ignoring what others are doing. I am good at making decisions that help me.

SAMPLE WRITING ASSIGNMENT D: TEACHER-SELECTED TOPIC

Have the students write sentences or paragraphs of their own. Have them include the problem behavior and other more appropriate choices. Have them end the assignment with at least one positive statement about their ability to handle things in the future.

IGNORING

Some students respond best to being ignored when they are being inappropriate. The class can be encouraged to assist with this intervention by being awarded bonus points or small treats for ignoring inappropriate behavior. Be quick to give the student plenty of attention when his or her behavior becomes appropriate.

This intervention is not the best one for students who are extremely physically aggressive.

OVERPRACTICE

For students who deface property, throw food, urinate on the floor and walls, or knock furniture over, over-practice will often get their attention. Basically all this involves is having the students clean up the mess they made and then do more cleaning to practice the new skill. A student who throws food in the lunchroom can be expected to mop the whole cafeteria floor and wipe off all cafeteria tables. While the student is doing this, he or she should receive little or no attention. The adult who is monitoring the student should refrain from scolding, nagging, or chatting. This is not a social time. When the student is finished, praise for a job well done is appropriate.

INDIVIDUAL CONTRACTS

This intervention requires careful planning and should be used only after other classroom procedures have failed. Individual contracts describe in specific, observable terms the inappropriate behaviors the student exhibits, and the desired behaviors, educative strategies, proactive interventions, punishments, and rewards that will be implemented in response to a student's choices. A form should be filled out with this information, and all parties involved should sign it.

Formal functional behavioral assessments should include baseline data, a method for continuing to document behaviors of concern, a hypothesis for the function of the target behavior, and strategies that directly address the function of the behavior. If a student is exhibiting a particular behavior because he wants to avoid work, for example, and the teacher sends the student to the office where he is not required to complete his work, the student will probably continue to act in ways that get him sent to the office. Going to the office is a reinforcer, not a punisher because the student does not want to do work.

For more information on how to conduct individual functional behavioral assessments, go to the following websites:

Positive Behavior Intervention and Support   www.pbis.com

Florida Department of Education   www.firn.edu/doe

Note: Do not use exclusion from school without the parent's knowledge or if the student really would rather be at home.

HIERARCHY OF PUNISHMENTS

1. Verbal warning.

2. Mark on the chalkboard.

3. Three marks equal a "0" on the point sheet.

4. Cool-off. The student will sit in a chair or carrel removed from the activity area of the room. Points are earned here. Bonus points can be earned for going without being told to avoid a problem. Time in cool-off is short.

5. In-class suspension. The student will sit in a chair or carrel as far away from other activities as possible. No points are earned here—Work can be done if the student is calm enough. Time in this area is longer.

6. Time-out. The student will sit in a chair or carrel outside the classroom if possible. No points are earned here. No classwork is done here. Time in this area is variable. Students do not return to the class until they do whatever time they were told to do in in-class suspension first.

7. Exclusion from school by being sent home or by serving some kind of in-school suspension program if it is available.

HIERARCHY OF REWARDS

1. Verbal praise.

2. Points on the point sheet.

3. Edible rewards.

4. Tangible rewards that are not edible.

5. Certificates.

6. Bonus points.

7. Classroom store.

8. "Student of the Week" award.

9. Recognition in class or school-wide for some achievement.

10. Special activity period.

11. Permission to visit other classes or staff members.

12. Permission to run errands for the teacher.

13. Assignment as classroom helper.

14. Assignment as office helper.

SAMPLE CONTRACT

1. Problem Behaviors

      a. Refuses to do work.

      b. Leaves room without permission.

      c. Screams and curses at classmates and teachers.

      d. Urinates on wails and the floor in the time-out area.

2. Function Hypothesis

When math, reading, and writing assignments are given, the student refuses to complete the assignment, screams and curses at staff and peers, leaves the room without permission, and urinates on the wall and floor of the time-out room.

3. Desired Behavior

      a. Complete one half of the math assignment before getting breakfast. Complete math before going to PE. Complete at least one other morning assignment before getting lunch.

      b. Ask permission before leaving the room. Stay in the room and discuss the problem with the teacher or sit quietly.

      c. Talk appropriately to the teacher and classmates.

      d. Complete time-out in an appropriate manner.

4. Educative Strategies

Increase compliance with academic tasks by increasing academic skills.

      a. Teach multiplication facts systematically to accelerate mastery

            1. Os, 1s, 2s, and 5s

            2. 9s using fingers

            3. Commutative Property

      b. Teach word patterns and sight words to mastery before giving the student a reading passage in a textbook

      c. Teach the student to use graphic organizers prior to writing a paragraph

5. Proactive Strategies

Increase compliance with academic tasks by providing the student with preferred materials for work completion.

      a. Provide computer program game formats for drill and practice

      b. Provide markers and chart paper for illustrating graphic organizers

6. Rewards

     a. Eat breakfast and lunch on time with the rest of the class.

     b. Go to PE on time with the rest of the class.

     c. Visit another staff member of the student's choice to show that staff member the completed work and receive a small, edible reward.

     d. Join classmates in special activity periods.

     e. Earn a weekly cooking activity.

     f. Avoid in-class suspension and time-out.

     g. Remain in school.

     h. Receive a special edible reward at the end of each day that the student talks appropriately to teachers and peers.

7. Punishments

     a. No food or PE until above-stated assignments are completed.

     b. Time-out and a loss of one special activity period each time the student leaves the room without permission.

     c. In-class suspension for talking inappropriately to teachers and peers (5 minutes for each inappropriate comment).

     d. The student will wash the entire time-out area each time he urinates in it. All walls and the floor will be scrubbed.

     e. Exclusion from school for the remainder of the day if the student refuses to follow this contract.

8. Signatures

Student _____

Teacher _____

Parent _____

Any Other Staff Member(s) Involved

_____

_____

BLANK CONTRACT

1. Problem Behaviors

2. Function Hypothesis

3. Desired Behavior

4. Educative Strategies

5. Proactive Strategies

6. Rewards

7. Punishments

8. Signatures

Student _____ Date _____
Teacher _____
Parent _____

Any Other Staff Member(s) Involved
_____
_____
_____

Date to Review the Plan _____

SUGGESTED AFFECTIVE EDUCATION MATERIALS

Social Skills

- *Skillstreaming the Elementary School Child (McGinnis & Goldstein)*
- *Skillstreaming the Adolescent (Goldstein)*
- *Social Skills for Special Children (Mannix)*

Cognitive-Behavioral

- *Thinking, Feeling, Behaving Grades 1-6 (Vernon)*
- *Thinking, Feeling, Behaving Grades 7-12 (Vernon)*
- *Thinking, Changing, Rearranging (Anderson)*
- *Positively! Learning to Manage Negative Emotions (Kerr)*

Selected Stories, Films, & Other Instructional Resources

- *Primary (Grades 1 - 3)*
- *On Monday When It Rains by Cherryl Kachenmeister (Identifying feelings)*
- *Knots on a Counting Rope by Bill Martin, Jr. & John Archambault (Coping with loss)*
- *Let's Be Enemies by Janice May Udry (Conflict with a friend)*
- *The Island of Skog by Steven Kellogg (Fear of the unknown & conflict resolution)*
- *The Hating Book by Charlotte Zolotow (Conflict with a friend)*
- *The Fight by Betty Boegehold (Conflict & consequences)*
- *An American Tale*
- *The Butter Battle*
- *The Wizard of OZ*

Intermediate (Grades 4 - 5)

- *"The King and His Hawk" in The Children's Book of Virtues by W. J. Bennett (Anger)*
- *Hope by Isabell Monk (Pride in cultural heritage & overcoming prejudice)*
- *Crazy Lady by Jane Leslie Conly (Conflict resolution & overcoming disabilities)*
- *Chicken Sunday by Patricia Polacco (Love, friendship, & overcoming prejudice)*
- *The True Story of the Three Little Pigs by Jon Scieszka (Alternative perspectives in a conflict)*
- *On My Honor by Marion Dane Bauer (Dealing with loss & conscience)*
- *What Jamie Saw by Carolyn Coman (Dealing with domestic abuse)*
- *October Sky*
- *Where the Red Fern Grows*
- *Charlie and the Chocolate Factory*

Secondary

- *The Hatchet by G. Paulsen   (Coping with loss and problem-solving)*
- *That Was Then This Is Now by S. E. Hinton*
  (Conflict: Loyalty to a friend or to personal goals)
- *Call of the Wild by Jack London (Conflict and coping with loss)*
- *A Girl Named Disaster by Nancy Farmer (Coping, loss, and survival)*
- *People Profiles   (Series: Biographies of famous people)*
- *Rudy*
- *Dangerous Minds*
- *Apollo 13*

ADDITIONAL INSTRUCTIONAL RESOURCES & REFERENCES

Bernard, M. (1990). *Rational-emotive therapy with children and adolescents: Treatment strategies. School Psychology Review, 19(3), 294-303.*

Campbell, L. A. (1999). *Storybooks for tough times. Golden, CO: Fulcrum Publishing.*

Center for Applied Psychology. (n.d.). *Face it! King of Prussia, PA.*

Cummings, C. (1996). *The get-alongs. Edmonds, WA: Teaching, Inc.*

Cummings, C., & Haggerty, K. (1997). *Raising healthy children. Educational Leadership, 54(8), 28-30.*

DiGiuseppe, R., & Bernard, M. (1990). *The application of rational-emotive theory and therapy to school-aged children. School Psychology Review, 19(3), 268-286.*

Ellis, A., & Harper, R. (1975). *A new guide to rational living. Hollywood, CA: Wilshire Book.*

Hesley, J. W., & Hesley, J. G. (1998). *Rent two movies and let's talk in the morning. New York, NY: John Wiley & Sons, Inc.*

Kerr, R. (1997). *Positively! Learning to manage negative emotions. Portland, ME: J. Weston Walsh.*

Kidder, R., & Born, P. (1999). *Resolving ethical dilemmas in the classroom. Educational Leadership, 56(4), 38-41.*

Kupper, L. (1994). (Ed.). *A guide to children's literature and disability. Washington, DC: NICHCY.*

Mannix, D. (1993). *Social skills activities for special children. West Nyack, NY: The Center for Applied Research.*

Nichols, P. (1998). *Teaching thinking skills—A class act. Beyond Behavior, 9(1), 12-19.*

Richards, J., & Standley, M. (1982). *Dealing with feelings. Santa Barbara, CA: The Learning Works.*

Schmidt, F. & Friedman, A. (1985). *Creative conflict solving for kids. Miami, FL: Grace Contrino Abrams Peace Education Foundation, Inc.*

Shure, M. (1992). I can problem solve: An interpersonal cognitive problem solving program. Champaign, IL: Research Press.

Seligman, M. (1996). The optimistic child. New York, NY: Harper Perennial.

Serna, L. A., & Lau-Smith, J. A. (1995). Learning with a purpose: Self-determination skills for students who are at risk for school and community failure. Intervention in School and Clinic, 30, 142-146.

Stoodt-Hill, B., & Amspaugh-Corson, L. (2001). Children's literature: Discovery for a lifetime, 2nd ed. Upper Saddle River, NJ: Merrill Prentice-Hall.

Vernon, A. (1989a). Thinking, feeling, behaving, 1-6. Champaign, IL: Research Press.

Vernon, A. (1989b). Thinking, feeling, behaving, 7-12. Champaign, IL: Research Press.

Appendix J

QUICK-REFERENCE CHECKLISTS FOR INTERVENTION STRATEGIES

PASSIVE AGGRESSIVE PERSONALITY

Distinguishing Behaviors

_____   Habitually slow to start or stop an activity on time.

_____   Often "forgets" to follow directions, but rarely forgets favored activities.

                    Encouragement in the form of reminding the student of pending punishments as well as rewards produces even slower performance and less compliance.

_____   Does little that is really "bad" but manages to alienate his or her peers.

_____   Drops things, loses things, looks for things, suddenly needs to use the restroom or get a drink just as the class gets settled and ready to listen.

Interventions

_____   Don't nag and remind. Ignore as much inappropriate behavior as possible.

_____   If the student can read, supply him or her with a list of rules, rewards, and consequences in writing. Use picture symbols if the student cannot read. Tape it to the student's desk or bulletin board space.

_____   Failure to comply within a predetermined time will equal a punishment. Compliance will equal a reward.

_____   Give instructions one time. Be specific.

_____   Without nagging or discussing it further, follow through on the consequences.

_____   When the student wants to discuss how he or she forgot or couldn't really help it, respond that you are aware of how people sometimes make mistakes, but that the consequences are the same. Be matter of fact.

_____   Don't show anger.

_____   Don't accept excuses.

ATTENTION DEFICIT DISORDER

DISTINGUISHING BEHAVIORS

_____ Is fidgety.
_____ Is off task often.
_____ Interrupts own train of thought with off-the-topic comments.
_____ Starts but rarely finishes things.
_____ Is always busy but never gets anywhere with it.
_____ Gets loud and over-stimulated easily.
_____ Sometimes escalates to physical aggression.
_____ Talks out; is talkative.
_____ Is unorganized.
_____ Wanders.
_____ Is easily confused by too many directions at once.
_____ Is distractible.

INTERVENTIONS

_____ Divide assignments into two parts whenever possible. Reward the student for each half completed.
_____ Provide the student with self-structuring activities.
_____ Have an "office" area for this student to use during independent work times. This area is not to be used as a punishment. It is a special area with few visual distractions meant to help the student stay focused.
_____ Put clothespins on a line. The student moves the clothespins each time an assignment is completed. A new assignment is not to be started until the first is finished.
_____ Send the student on errands as a reward for completion of work. This student needs to move occasionally.
_____ Praise for what is done works better than reminders to finish. Say, "I see that you have already completed five items! This is great! I can't wait to see the next five! Please raise your hand when you finish them so I can come to see what you have done."
_____ Watch the student's schedule for too much activity or too much time with nothing to do.
_____ Raise your own hand to remind a student who is interrupting to raise his or her hand and wait to be called on. Don't talk to the student until his or her hand is raised.
_____ Refuse to talk to the student unless he or she is in the assigned area. Turn your back if the student walks up to you. Say, "I only talk to people who are in their seats." When the student sits, turn around and walk toward him or her.

Websites of interest for teachers and parents of students with ADHD—

LD Online
www.ldonline.com

Children and Adults with Attention Deficit Disorder
www.chadd.org

CONDUCT DISORDER

DISTINGUISHING BEHAVIORS

_____ Has little respect for authority.
_____ Uses profanity profusely.
_____ Often talks about fighting.
_____ Is quick to anger.
_____ Often misunderstands others' intentions.
_____ Active play often becomes over-stimulating, resulting in fighting.
_____ Is impulsive.
_____ Is explosive.
_____ Has low tolerance for frustration.
_____ Throws items.
_____ Spits, kicks, hits, bites, urinates on people or school items.
_____ Vandalizes.
_____ Is sensitive to issues of fairness only if related to his or her own consequences.
_____ May leave assigned area without permission (i.e., run away).

INTERVENTIONS

_____ Actively enforce the rule that people are not for hurting
_____ Send a clear message that physical assaults will not be tolerated.
_____ Take extra care to be *consistent* with the student.
_____ Structure academic assignments for maximum opportunities for success.
_____ Carefully monitor peer interactions.
_____ Send the student on an errand (even if it is only to deliver a message to the office that says, "Just take this and say Thanks.") to get him or her out of a potentially overwhelming situation before things get out of hand.
_____ Tell the student how much you appreciate his or her self-control even in the midst of a problem. It may seem silly to compliment a student who has thrown every book in his or her desk across the room for not attempting to hurt anyone. However, students with conduct disorders do not trust adults. They often feel that the teacher is only there to punish. *Constant* reminders of appropriate decision making, even in the midst of a problem, help them feel more trusting of the teacher, and they also help them get in touch with their own ability to handle them selves appropriately.
_____ Give the student extra bonus points or an edible reward for going to the cool-off area on his or her own to avoid a problem.
_____ Reward the student specifically for handling problems in the classroom without running away.
_____ Whenever possible, ignore comments made to discount compliments made about the student's appropriate behavior.
_____ Don't overreact to profanity and disrespectful comments. Spending five minutes in the cool-off area for each curse word is sufficient.

DEPRESSION/SUICIDAL TENDENCIES

DISTINGUISHING BEHAVIORS

_____   May be withdrawn.
_____   May be aggressive.
_____   May be whiney and clinging.
_____   May daydream excessively.
_____   May give up without trying.
_____   May seem lethargic.
_____   May seem tense.
_____   May cry easily.
_____   May express exaggerated fears.

INTERVENTIONS

_____   Structure academic assignments for success. Encourage participation with rewards.

_____   Be matter of fact when reassuring the student about a fear. Take the fear seriously, but don't take too much time with unnecessary explanations.

_____   Show the student real evidence of past successes.

_____   Help the student focus on decisions and actions that require immediate attention.

_____   Talk with the student about the importance of remembering that mistakes are a valuable part of learning. One little mistake can easily become an insurmountable obstacle without occasional reality input from others.

_____   Ask the student to listen to another, less capable student read. Give this student little jobs to reinforce positive feelings about himself or herself.

_____   Take any threats of suicide seriously. Get assistance from the school social worker, psychologist, or guidance counselor. Notify parents. DO NOT LEAVE THE STUDENT UNATTENDED.

_____   Do not let a student who has threatened suicide leave the room unescorted.

_____   Watch for any sudden mood changes. Even a change for the better could signal a problem if the change is unexplainable or sudden.

A valuable resource for educators is Eleanor Guetzloe's (1989) book, *Youth Suicide: What the Educator Should Know*, available through the Council for Exceptional Children.

PSYCHOTIC DISORDERS

DISTINGUISHING BEHAVIORS

_____   Evidence of hallucinations.

_____   Repetitive speech patterns.

_____   Repetitive behaviors that appear meaningless.

_____   Refusal to talk for extended periods of time.

_____   Periods when the student appears not to be able to hear.

_____   Reports from the student of people or creatures that do not exist for others, but do have some kind of control over this student.

_____   Extreme mood swings.

INTERVENTIONS

_____   Be consistent. This student needs predictable behavior from the teacher to help counteract the chaos in his or her own head.

_____   Keep schedules as stable as possible.

_____   Give the student plenty of warning and explanation if changes must be made. Always talk to the student as if he or she can understand. The student's behavior may not be a good indicator of when or how much he or she understands.

_____   Do not send the student on errands unless he or she is familiar with the school and is stable.

Keep in close contact with the parents. These students with psychotic disorders are often being seen by psychiatrists and are often on medication of some kind. Find out what medication the student is on. If the student shows signs of side effects or his or her behavior changes drastically, contact the parents. Written permission to talk with the doctor is usually required.